The West Yorkshire Way

Nicholas Parrott

Published by Sigma Leisure – an imprint of
Sigma Press, 1 South Oak Lane, Wilmslow, Cheshire SK9 6AR, England.

British Library Cataloguing in Publication Data
A CIP record for this book is available from the British Library.

ISBN: 1-85058-327-7

Typesetting and Design by: Sigma Press, Wilmslow, Cheshire.

Maps by: David Holdsworth

Text photographs: Nicholas Parrott

Cover photograph: Close Gate Bridge, near Marsden (Nicholas Parrott)

Printed and Bound by
Manchester Free Press, Unit E3, Longford Trading Estate, Thomas Street, Stretford, Manchester M32 0JT. Telephone 061 864 4540

General Disclaimer

Whilst every effort has been made to ensure that the information given in this book is correct, neither the publisher nor the author accept any responsibility for any inaccuracy.

Foreword

The last two decades have seen a great upsurge of interest in walking and in published routes. I've had the great pleasure of being involved in some of this, firstly as an 'enthusiastic amateur' and later as an equally enthusiastic Countryside Officer.

Exactly twenty years ago, in 1973, I attended the initial meeting of a group of local people from local Civic Trusts who had come together to create a Calderdale Way. This was to become Britain's first 'Recreational Path' designated under, what was then, a new Countryside Commission scheme. Later, at West Yorkshire Metropolitan County Council, I was involved in several path development schemes including Leeds County Way, Dearne Way, Wakefield Walkways and the early stages of Kirklees Way. Somewhere about 1986 I thought how interesting it would be to put parts of these (and other) routes together to make a complete circuit of the County. However, like many others who have bright ideas, I didn't do much about it beyond jotting down a few notes as to how it might be achieved.

Now Nicholas Parrott has produced his version of 'The Grand Tour' around West Yorkshire. I've been fascinated to see his idea develop and be refined into the version you now have before you.

This is a long walk, but it can be broken down into sections of varying lengths and I do suggest that the best way to tackle it is by using public transport. Those who are not use to buses and trains will find that there is plenty of expert advice and specialist literature available to tell you how to get from A to B etc. Do take your time along the way and savour the wide variety of countryside through which you'll pass. Its not for running around nor for competitive events! It is there to be walked steadily and enjoyed by those who know that West Yorkshire contains some fantastic scenery - and to convert those who hadn't yet realised that.

Happy Walking

David Nortcliffe.

CONTENTS

Acknowledgments

I should like to thank the many people who have helped and inspired me with this book. I am particularly grateful to: David Holdsworth, who has provided the excellent maps; Peta Hudson, who developed and printed the photos; and David Nortcliffe of Calderdale MBC who has made many helpful suggestions on the presentation and content of the book.

While researching this book, I have often needed to call upon footpath and countryside officers in local authorities. They have provided valuable assistance and advice. I would specifically like to thank the following individuals for their help: Mr Gibson (Barnsley MBC), Rick Hill (Bradford MBC), Roger Brookes (Leeds CC), Virginia Moulton and Paul Andrews (Wakefield CC), Kath Windebt (Kirkless MC) and John Adams and Mrs Renshaw (North Yorkshire County Council). Thanks are also due to British Waterways and British Coal (Opencast) for their cooperation in enabling the use of permissive rights of way along the route.

I should also like to thank Mr Beswick and his colleagues at Metro, Graham Beech and the staff at Sigma, and friends and colleagues who have offered their support throughout

Nicholas Parrott

For Harry, who introduced me
to the Pennine Hills and for Joy,
without whom the light would
shine less brightly

INTRODUCTION

This book outlines a new unofficial long-distance footpath, the West Yorkshire Way, a 150-mile walk around the borders of West Yorkshire. Unlike most other long distance routes, it is a walk that can be done in day stages. The starting and finishing point of each day being linked to the county's extensive and inexpensive public transport network.

The book is intended to appeal to a wide range of walkers, from the experienced trail walker to the afternoon rambler. The lengths of the walks vary from 6 to 20 miles, though most are between 10 and 15 miles long. On all but the shortest walks, there are opportunities to break the day's walk to give two shorter walks. Information on public transport links to the starting, finishing and intermediate points along each day's walk is provided in the text.

One reason for writing this book is to fill a gap in the guide books currently available. At one extreme there is the "easy walks from your car" type of book. By necessity, these walks always start and end in the same place and for many of us they lack a sense of adventure. At the other extreme there are what are often called "challenge walks", which while providing a sense of adventure, all too often turn into endurance tests.

The West Yorkshire Way presents the challenge of a long distance footpath without the endurance factor of backpacking and the feeling that the whole walk has to be done within a strict time limit. (This almost inevitably happens when you have 200 miles and two weeks holiday). It also means long distance walking without the bills for B&B or camping, or having a bag full of smelly socks.

It is possible to do the route over a fortnight or two weekly stages. For those who wish to do so, I have provided addresses of Tourist Information Centres, who can help with accommodation arrangements. For visitors to the county, it is surely as convenient to book accommodation in one of the larger towns and do the walk, or parts of it, in day stages. For those of us living within, or close to, West Yorkshire each walk can be managed within a day, giving time to get home for supper.

A second reason for writing this book is to encourage greater use of the public transport network. The route reaches some of the most remote parts of the County, yet it is all easily accessible by public transport. I hope that this book will encourage those of you with cars to leave them in the drive next time you go walking. It should also give those without cars new ideas for getting about.

Despite growing environmental awareness, many of us are unwilling to give up our cars because of the convenience that they offer. The government is unlikely to renege on its present road building policy, so the most effective contribution that we can make is to change our habits and, at least, reduce our dependency on the motor car. Whatever technological advances are made, increased ownership and greater use of cars for leisure mean that car emissions are rapidly becoming the largest single source of atmospheric pollution in the UK. Not only this but, as car use goes up, road congestion increases and more land is given over for new roads and car parks. At the time of writing, this route crosses one proposed motorway route (the M1 – M62 link), one trunk road being upgraded to a motorway (the A1) and one planned bypass (around South Elmshall).

The Walk

The West Yorkshire Way provides an opportunity to savour the great diversity of landscapes, countryside and architecture within the county. From the windswept moors in the west, to the rich rolling farmlands in the east, no two days of this walk are alike. As a circular walk there is no fixed starting or finishing point, but you can choose to do sections of the walk as and when it pleases you.

The book itself can logically be divided into four sections: the northern, eastern, southern and western edges of the county. There are three day walks along each of these sections, except the western one which will take four days to complete. The northern and southern sections are shorter (at 31 and 35 miles respectively) than the eastern and western sections (which are 42 and 43 miles respectively). The western section is the highest, much of it lying above 1000 feet, while the eastern section is the flattest. Each section has its own unique character and interest, which changes gradually as you move in each direction of the compass.

The Northern Section

The route starts in the north west of the county at Steeton, near Keighley. This northern section of the walk runs eastwards from here towards Wetherby, passing through Ilkley, Menston, Bramhope and Harewood on the way. We start by crossing the river Aire, just a few miles upstream of Bradford. The path runs along the broad, flat valley bottom before climbing steeply through grazing land onto Ilkley Moor. Once on the top of the moor, the views change dramatically as the expanse of the Wharfe Valley, and the soft green hills of the Yorkshire Dales open up to the north. The first day is a short one ending in the pretty town of Ilkley, on the banks of the Wharfe.

On the second day we climb back onto Ilkley Moor, passing through boulders and craggy outcrops to bring us onto the eastern side of the moor. Here we follow the route of both the Ebor Way and the Dales Way, contouring along the top of the moor. After a few miles the path drops to the valley below passing through farmland to Menston and then climbing back up to Guiseley Moor. From the top of the moor the path soon leads to the Chevin, a high ridge above Otley. This is a popular spot, maintained as a forest park by Leeds City Council, with woods, ponds and open downland close to one another. The path runs on towards the forestry plantations on the eastern side of the Chevin Forest Park to lead to the picturesque village of Bramhope, our second day's stop.

The third day is the longest day on the northern section running for some 15 miles from Bramhope to Wetherby. We are in the open rolling countryside of the Lower Wharfe for the whole of the day, sticking close to the route of the Ebor Way. Having dropped away from the higher slopes of the past two days, the views are not so spectacular. Yet, there is much of interest to be seen besides the lovely parkland and woodlands. During the day we pass a quarry with spectacular cliff faces, the stately home of Harewood, a nearby church tucked away in the woods and a monastery. In the afternoon there is a long and peaceful stretch along the banks of the Wharfe before arriving at Wetherby. Once a major stopping point on the A1 this town is full of charm and has an interesting old market place (Thursday is market day). Being some distance from the towns in the west of the county, it may be a good place for a weekend. There is plenty of B&B accommodation and a camp site.

The Eastern Section

The route turns southwards shortly after Wetherby and runs towards South Elmsall. Here we see a gradual progression from rich agricultural land to an area that was, until recently, heavily industrial. Yet, in the midst of this industrial land there is much beautiful countryside. Along the route pretty villages turn up in regular succession, from Thorpe Arch four miles past Wetherby to Wentbridge a few miles before South Elmsall. These villages were once all stopping off points on the Great North Road. As traffic levels grew in the post war years, bypasses were built around all of them and they have returned to their former serenity.

On the first day, we go eastwards from Wetherby for a few miles before crossing the narrow bridge over the Wharfe into Boston Spa, an old spa town on the banks of the river. Then we turn south leaving the Ebor Way for the last time. From here, we pick up parts of the Limestone Country Day Walks created by the former W.Y.M.C.C. We skirt around the village of Clifford whose Catholic Church, based on the design of Angouleme Cathedral in France, provides a prominent and interesting landmark. The village of Bramham provides a convenient lunchstop (or stopping point for those who prefer a shorter day's walk). Shortly after we enter the grounds of Bramham Park, "The Versailles of Yorkshire", famous for its gardens and follies. Rolling woodland and meadow follow leading towards Aberford, perhaps the most charming of villages on this eastern section. From Aberford there is a straight path through the forested grounds of the Parlington Estate to the edge of Garforth and the end of a long but rewarding day.

The second day leads from East Garforth through the newly expanded town of Kippax, and then out into more gently rolling woodland. This is a lovely day's walking, passing through the delightful village of Ledsham, with its medieval church and old pub. Later the walk goes through the RSPB reserve at Fairburn Ings, probably the most important bird reserve in West Yorkshire and a fine place for exploring. After Fairburn Ings the path follows the Aire downstream for a few miles to the old toll bridge at Ferrybridge. Along this stretch the power station is the dominant landmark growing closer and larger as the afternoon wears on. Past Ferrybridge, the last mile of the walk runs along a path between canal and river, recently restored by the Groundwork Trust, leading to the centre of Knottingley.

The last day's walk on this eastern section is in a little-visited corner of the county, passing into North Yorkshire for part of the day. Although this area is fairly flat, the small hills to be climbed afford views for miles around. There is a fair amount of road walking on this section, but the roads are all quiet and undisturbed by much traffic. Highlights of the day's walk include two pretty villages on opposite sides of the same valley, Kirk Smeaton and Little Smeaton. From here the footpath follows the tranquil valley of Brockadales, a Site of Special Scientific Interest, through to Wentbridge. From Wentbridge the path turns south again, passing through the villages of Thorpe Audlin and Upton before a steep drop into South Elmsall.

The Southern Section

Turning westwards from South Elmsall, the path ducks and weaves between West and South Yorkshire for the first couple of days on this, the southern section of the route. Although the first day is not the prettiest along the route, there is much of interest. We pass several collieries, all now closed, some now landscaped. We also cross many disused railway lines, many of which provide us with our route. Despite the industrial heritage of this area, there is much farmland, open ground and open views. The route takes us through several towns and villages, including Hemsworth, Brierley, Shafton and Royston; all are free from the trappings of tourism and have their own varied and distinct charm. Near the end of the day we are rewarded with sweeping views of Barnsley and its surrounding and surprisingly green countryside.

The second two days of this section are days of anticipation as we sense the approach of the Pennines and the growing steepness and frequency of hills. Leaving Darton, the path follows the meanderings of the Dearne (and the Dearne Way) along a lovely stretch of water meadows and farmland towards the hamlet of Haigh. From Haigh we start to rise across open parkland which provides views across Bretton Park. Reaching the crest of the hill we enter Kirklees for the first time and are rewarded with extensive views across the Pennine foothills. From here the path drops into Clayton West, and climbs steeply back up towards High Hoyland, which affords extensive views across the South Yorkshire tops. From High Hoyland we traverse more hills on the way to Bagden Park and a final stretch through wooded country along the top of the steep sides of the Dearne Valley. Denby Dale with its magnificent viaduct stands near the head of the valley

From Denby Dale the country continues to grow ever more hilly and the day begins by climbing to Bird's Edge, close to the source of the Dearne. Around Bird's Edge there are very few footpaths and we are obliged to stick to minor roads for a few miles. Soon these are left behind and we are rewarded with narrow paths skirting around the edge of Cheese Gate Nab before dropping to the steep valley around Jackson Bridge and Hepworth. The former of these villages has a mill discreetly tucked away in the valley bottom, the walk passing the mill shop. Shortly after there is the pleasant surprise of following the trail through the deeply notched valley that is Morton Wood. This fertile and moist valley runs off the edge of Scholes Moor and provides a contrast to the moors which are to follow. Two more stretches of moorland punctuated by two valleys (now dammed as reservoirs) will eventually lead to Holme. Both these valleys have unusually attractive stretches of conifers planted around their reservoirs, with good paths leading through them.

The final section around Ramsden Reservoir is particularly inspiring. Situated on the very edge of the Peak District National Park, the scenery is reminiscent of Scotland. The edges of the forest tumble down to the still waters below, and the path crosses several fast running streams. Emerging from the forest the path climbs the last hundred feet or so up to Holme; this is a beautiful village surrounded by bleak moorland, and the last settlement before the pass over Holme Moss leading to Derbyshire.

The Western Section

At almost 1000 ft, Holme provides a suitably high starting point for the high level route along the Pennines which will complete the circuit back to Steeton. From here the path turns northwards and out onto the high moors. Each day on this western section follows a similar pattern of rising from a town or village, then passing through grazing land onto the tops and crossing these before descending to the next valley. On a wet day, civilisation can seem far away and protective clothing on these high sections is essential.

The first day leads us over farmland towards a bridge between two reservoirs. From here the path climbs up along Marsden Clough towards Wessenden Head. Crossing the road here we follow one track all the way down to Marsden, passing a series of reservoirs along the bottom of this high level valley. Splendid rocky outcrops and fast running streams provide pleasure and interest along the route. Marsden itself is a typical Pennine town nestled in a bowl of hills at the top of the Colne Valley. It grew both as a textile town and as a staging post on Huddersfield – Oldham routes.

Leaving Marsden on the next stage, the route passes an important part of this legacy: Tunnel End. This marks one end of Standedge Tunnel; completed in 1811, this three-mile tunnel was the longest and highest tunnel on the entire British canal network until its closure nearly 50 years ago. Beyond the tunnel end the path climbs back up onto the moors. After two miles it rejoins the Pennine Way and leads across some of the highest and bleakest moorland in the country. At the half way point during the day, the M62 is crossed by an awesomely high footbridge. The motorway is set in a deep cutting here, and is only audible when you get close to it and is soon left behind.

Shortly after the motorway bridge the path climbs almost imperceptibly towards Blackstone Edge, the highest point on the entire West Yorkshire Way which is, ironically, just outside the county boundary. This long shelf of exposed gritstone is one of the more famous landmarks on the Pennine Way. It is said that Roman legionnaires used to pass by here on their way across the tops of the moors. For many of them it must have seemed a long way from the sweeter climes of home. We continue along the Pennine way for some distance yet, passing the welcoming White House on the Halifax – Rochdale road, and a series of high level reservoirs that lead into the edge of Calderdale. After 10 miles of high level walking the path turns westwards at the edge of the last of these reservoirs and leads off the moors to the small village of Walsden. From Walsden there is a delightful walk along the canal towpath to

Todmorden. This town probably has the best selection of restaurants and pubs along the entire route, and is well worth lingering in at the end of the day.

In the recent past, Pennine towns and villages such as Todmorden, Marsden and some of the smaller settlements that we pass through seemed to have a dismal future. High rates of out-migration, unemployment and a legacy of declining industries were beginning to take their toll. (Haworth, with its Brontë connection, has always been something of an exception to this). Now, although some of those problems remain, these towns and villages are seeing a reversal in their fortunes. They are becoming desirable places to live and are popular with day trippers. Once this process has begun, it can create its own problems and may detract from the original character of a town, filling the streets with little but tea rooms and antique shops. Todmorden appears to have started along this process, yet it still retains its strong local identity. For the time being, at least, it is striking a balance between the two extremes.

The day that starts from Todmorden is one of the longest sections of the West Yorkshire Way and it also involves a considerable amount of ascent. There are convenient points to turn off to Hebden Bridge for those who feel that the walk is too much for one day. This area is criss-crossed with footpaths, many of which are flagged and were originally used by mill workers or, in earlier times, as pack horse routes.

After a steep climb from Todmorden, the route links up to the Calderdale Way and follows it through Blackshawhead to Colden Clough. On the far side of Colden Clough, it turns off onto the Pennine Way for a short stretch to Green Hill. From here we are on lesser used local footpaths, which lead to the top of Hardcastle Crags. This steep-sided wooded valley, fed by waters from the moors, is a nationally famous beauty spot. Our route cuts straight across the valley, up the punishingly-steep far side and on up to Walshaw Lodge. From here it skirts around the edge of the moor to link with the old road between Hebden Bridge and Haworth. This leads across wild moorland before descending into the top of the Worth Valley near Oxenhope. From here the path leads alongside the river Worth (and close to the steam powered Worth Valley Railway Line) to Haworth.

The last day of the West Yorkshire Way, takes us through the centre of Brontë Country, up the old cobbled High Street of Haworth and past the old parsonage before getting into open countryside. This section of the walk is on lower ground than the previous three, running across the tops of farmland rather than the wilderness of moors. Passing through the villages of Newsholme, Goose Eye and Laycock, it contains a wealth of interesting industrial archeology and stunning countryside. Rising over the hills above Laycock, the shapes of the southern peaks of the Yorkshire Dales (including Pen-y-Ghent) come into view. Descending from this hilltop brings us back to our starting point at Steeton, and the opportunity to celebrate the completion of a round of 150 miles of the best of West Yorkshire.

The Story behind the Book

When I was talking to a friend about writing this book, she asked where the original idea came from. Initially it came from looking at a poster of the Metro train network, while planning my next walk. I realised that I had visited about a third of the outlying stations on the network, and each had offered great walking opportunities. Perhaps a route linking all of these stations would make for some interesting new excursions.

Three years on, the West Yorkshire Way is now a reality. Some routes were easy to plan, with an obvious choice of direct paths. Quite frequently these paths have already been designated as parts of other walks such as the Ebor, Pennine and Calderdale Ways. As such they are usually well maintained and signposted. Other paths on the route are those used by local people in their daily comings and goings. These are mostly well-trod, though tend to be less well signposted. In some places there is such a profusion of footpaths that I was spoilt for choice. This was particularly true in the Calder and Worth Valleys. In other sections, especially in the east, the lack of footpaths and the existence of large private estates meant, on occasion, pushing the walk out beyond the boundaries of West Yorkshire and staying on roads longer than was initially envisaged.

Some changes to the original idea of a route linking all the outlying stations to the Metro network have been made for practical reasons and these are outlined below. Yet, mostly, the book remains true to this original idea.

Some towns or villages not on the rail network have been included as starting and stopping points on the walk for reasons of convenience and practicality. Holme, at the top of the Holme valley is included because the walk from Denby Dale to Marsden is too long for most people to complete in one day. For similar reasons, Oxenhope in the Worth Valley is included as a break between Todmorden and Steeton. This also provides a good excuse to travel on the privately-run Worth Valley Railway Line from Keighley. Wetherby is included to take the walk away from the suburbs of Leeds and up into the countryside in the north eastern corner of the county.

The most glaring omission that train buffs will notice is that of Horsforth, the last station on the Leeds – Harrogate line. Initially I intended to take the walk into Horsforth, but found that this made the days from Ilkley and to Wetherby quite long. It also involved a significant detour from the line of the rest of the northern route, which for most of its length stays close to the county boundary, following the Ebor Way. Eventually I decided to substitute Bramhope for Horsforth and retain the line of the northern route. At least the Harrogate line passes directly under the village.

Micklefield, the last station on the York bound line has also been omitted and East Garforth substituted for it. Here the problems were twofold: the route into Micklefield would have been at the end of a very long day from Wetherby (which passes the station at East Garforth) and would have run parallel to the railway line into Micklefield. I felt it was unlikely that anyone would wish to continue for the extra three kilometres to catch the same train back. On the way out of Micklefield the most attractive route leads across the A1, at a point where there is neither footbridge nor tunnel for protection. Extensive roadworks are also due to begin here, as part of the process of upgrading the A1 to motorway status. Caution prevailed, from both concern about safety and possible future blocked paths and I opted for East Garforth.

Finally, in two cases outlying stations were downgraded from "starting point" status, although the walk still passes through them. Having walked the sections of the route that were to start and end in Walsden and Oxenhope, it seemed preferable to move the finishing point, down along their respective valleys to Todmorden and Haworth. Both are larger settlements, offering more frequent public transport connections and a wider choice of services. The approach to both towns is a gentle one along either canal or river, which seemed better suited to the end, than the start, of a long day.

For my part, walking and writing the West Yorkshire Way has been a journey of discovery around my adopted home county. I was already familiar with some of the areas, but there were others I had never before thought about visiting. Each day brought surprises, both scenically and in terms of understanding the social life and history of the area. I hope that you enjoy walking it as much as I have enjoyed writing it and discovering the hidden treasures of the county.

HOW TO USE THIS BOOK

The book is divided into thirteen chapters, each of which describes a day stage of the walk. These stages are not fixed and you can extend a walk to include part of the next one, or shorten one according to your taste. They are designed to give the easiest possible access to public transport, so if you are going to extend or shorten a walk do look to see where the next public transport link lies. On some days these are few and far between.

Each day's route gives details of the distance, ascent and approximate times for completion of each walk. Information about public transport links, availability of refreshments and the maps that you would need to cover the route are also included. Hopefully you will not need maps, as David Holdsworth's excellent sketch maps should prevent you from going astray. For those who feel happier with a map in their pack, details of the maps required are given in both the 2cm to 1km (Landranger) and the more detailed 4cm to 1km (Pathfinder) series are given. Loan copies of the 1:50000 series are available from many public libraries.

As for walking times, well, we all walk at different speeds and the times that I took to cover each route are at the low end of the range given at the start of each chapter. The best way to judge how closely these times approximate yours is through experience and by comparing your walking time to those given in the book.

Throughout the text, cumulative distances for each day's walk are given in brackets at relevant points. These figures are given in kilometres, rather than miles. The intention is not to confuse the reader, but to make life easier. The grid squares overlaid on all OS maps are kilometre squares. It is therefore easier to relate distance walked on the ground to that depicted on the map by thinking in kilometres than in miles. Orienteers have been thinking this way for some time simply because it is more reliable. As a rule-of-thumb guide, (which is accurate to 1%) 4km equals 2.5ml, which for many people is equivalent to one hour's steady walking.

Follow The Countryside Code

❏ Enjoy the countryside and respect its life and work

❏ Fasten all gates

❏ Guard against all risk of fire

❏ Keep your dogs under close control

❏ Keep to public paths across farmland

❏ Use gates and stiles to cross fences, hedges and walls

❏ Leave livestock, crops and machinery alone

❏ Take your litter home with you

❏ Help to keep all water clean

❏ Protect wildlife plants and trees

❏ Take special care on countryside roads

❏ Make no unnecessary noise

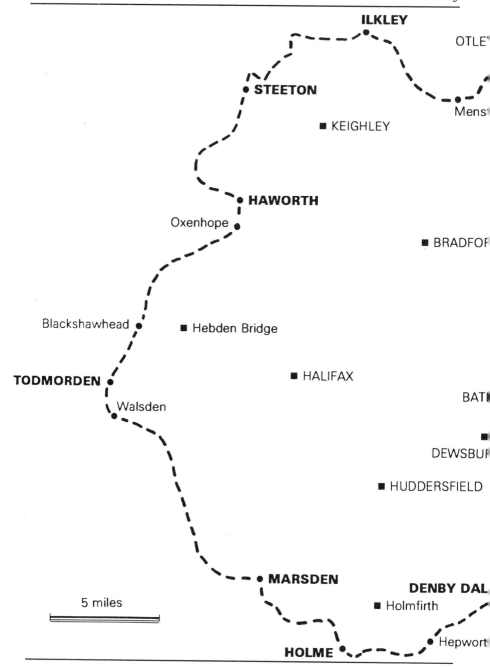

Northern Section – Walk One

Steeton to Ilkley

Route: Steeton – Howden House – Holden Beck – Doubler Stones – Rombalds Moor – Ilkley

Distance: 10km; 6.5ml

Time: 3 – 4$^1/_2$ hr

Ascent: 300m; 950ft

OS Maps: 1:25000 Pathfinder 671 Keighley & Ilkley; 1:50000 Landranger 104 Leeds, Bradford and Harrogate

Getting There

Steeton and Silsden is the last "cheap fares" station on the Airedale line, which then continues up towards Skipton and Settle. Trains run from both Leeds and Bradford (Forster Square). From Leeds trains run half hourly on Mondays to Saturdays and hourly on Sundays. From Bradford they run hourly on Mondays to Saturdays and two hourly on Sundays. There is also a bus link from Ilkley to Steeton. For details of getting back from Ilkley, see the next chapter.

The Day Ahead

This is quite a short walk which can easily be done in a half day, allowing time for an extended lunch and exploration around Ilkley, or to continue along part of the next section to Menston. It includes one of the finest waterfalls in West Yorkshire, in Howden Clough, and a traverse of one of the most spectacular ridges in the county which provides magnificent views across the Wharfe Valley. This ridge walk is popular

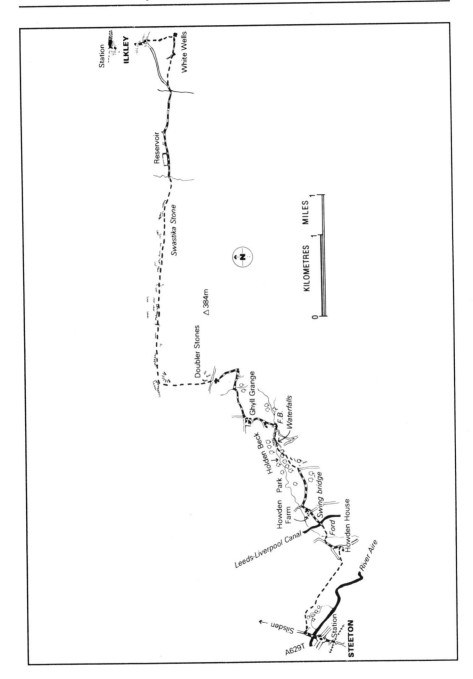

with ramblers at weekends, so can sometimes get crowded in peak season. There is much to explore in Ilkley which was once Yorkshire's premier spa resort, and still maintains much of its genteel atmosphere. Ilkley also has the bonus having the county's only public open air swimming pool.

Like many walks in this book (and elsewhere), the first mile or so is the hardest to explain since it involves following tracks and paths through farmland, until the path grows clearer on the uplands. Once on the higher ground, the paths are clear and easy to follow.

Waterfall in Howden Clough

From Steeton and Silsden BR

Leave the station and go right up the flight of steps to the road above and then right again along the road towards the roundabout. Cross the dual carriageway and carry straight on towards Silsden. The road takes you over the River Aire. Just after this bridge turn right onto the signposted footpath that leads over a tiny stone bridge, wide enough only for pedestrians. This leads to a field and then towards a raised track. Cross this and immediately cross the next bridge over a small beck. From here the path leads to a gap in the wall ahead. The rapidly expanding village of Silsden is seen ahead, with Rombalds Moor rising behind. To the right, on the other side of the valley the silhouette of Cliffe Castle is above the trees.

Once through the gap in the wall, follow the raised footpath to the right, until the path begins to turn away from the fence, following the beck around to the right. Carry straight on, dropping from the raised path and following the fence along, heading towards the stile in the corner of the hedge ahead. After the hedge, veer right, passing through a gate, and then turn left, follow the dry stone wall along to a gate and then over two stiles which you cross in quick succession. Keep close to the fence on your left, and the path leads to another gap in the wall. From here, the large buildings of Howden House appear. Head towards these, passing over one more stile and then following the path around the buildings, keeping them to your right hand side. The large building that the path passes was little more than a ruined shell as recently as the spring of 1991; it is now being comprehensively rebuilt. In a few minutes this path comes out onto a minor metalled road (1.5km).

Turn left onto the road and then go through the third gate on the right. Follow the path towards the bank, crossing a small ford on the way. Once on top of the bank the path swings to the left, towards some farm buildings. Before reaching these, the path crosses a swing bridge over the Leeds-Liverpool Canal. Here you might see brightly coloured narrow boats wending their way towards the Dales or Leeds. From the canal the path continues through the farm buildings and past a couple of cottages to a metalled road. Turn right here and go steeply uphill for 500m, the hardest climb of the day. Near the top, the road turns sharply to the right, go left here onto the signposted bridleway (2.5km)

This leads onto more open land with better views and clearly defined paths. Follow the bridleway uphill for 200m to a clear fork, just below some woods. This split in the track is indicated by painted markers on a stone. Follow the yellow and red markers onto the lower path and start to descend gently into the wooded valley on the left. Spectacular views into the bottom of Holden Beck are soon revealed. In May, the valley bottom below is awash with a carpet of bluebells. The path soon starts to rise again through the woodlands and after 300m there is another junction. A short detour can be made from here to the waterfalls at the bottom of this clough by following the steep staircase down the hillside into the valley bottom.

The West Yorkshire Way continues from the top of these steps, following the path that winds along the top of the valley. The sounds of the waterfalls below accompany your steps along the top of the valley. A series of yellow circles and red dots mark the twists in the path, over a couple of stone walls before emerging into a broader valley. Here, a footbridge, ford and pair of large concrete pillars carrying a water pipe cross the river (3.5km).

Cross the stream and follow the arrow painted on the far concrete pillar which points directly uphill. The steep incline soon slackens and the next marker becomes visible on the stone wall ahead. Turn right and follow the markers up to the gate and then go left up towards the farmhouse ahead (Ghyll Grange). Ignore the yellow marker pointing you to the left, instead go between the buildings and through the farmyard to emerge onto a concrete drive by the farmhouse.

Turn right here and follow this drive uphill for 100m until it gives way to a rough surfaced track. Follow this along over four cattle grids. At the fourth grid, turn off the track and follow the red and yellow markers uphill alongside a dry stone wall. After a short while this path turns almost 120 degrees to the left, following another dry stone wall uphill to Doubler Stone Farm, the highest farm on the moor. Follow the track through the farmyard and then out to the concrete drive beyond. This leads to a T-junction with another concrete drive, with a small bungalow to the left. Yellow dots on the rocks ahead act as guides across this open tract of rocky moorland. After a short while the Doubler Stones appear above on the right hand side (5km).

These are a remarkable pair of stones resembling, on first glimpse, cobblers' lasts: their smooth lines contrast strongly with their gritty rough texture. Their unusual shape is believed to a result of the last ice age. The more eroded sections at the bottom are affected by glacial erosion, the broader tops just remaining above the tops of the glacier.

One of the Doubler Stones

From Doubler Stones there is a clear path that continues rising towards the ridge above. This is heather moorland, splendid when in flower in high summer. A line of shooting hides can also be seen from the path, showing that walkers are not the only ones to be drawn here for their recreation. Ahead the path rises to a single stile over a marvellously straight and well-maintained dry stone wall, which rivals any in Lakeland. Some 200m further on, you find yourself on top of the ridge overlooking Wharfedale.

Here, you bid farewell to the yellow markers that have guided you to the top and turn to the right. From here it is a straight forward walk descending gently downhill all the way into Ilkley (about 4km further on). The track is well-cairned and provides one of the loveliest walks in the area. There are fine views all around, especially to the north, and an impressive series of crags falls away on your left hand side.

Descending towards Ilkley the path crosses many stiles which become more frequent as it draws closer to the town. At one point the path drops into a pasture with a large boulder in the middle and exotic looking conifers around, resembling a garden from Japanese paintings. Soon after the path crosses a beck and runs next to a small reservoir, before running alongside a dry stone wall, with houses behind it. After a 0.5km the wall ends, the path crosses another beck and comes out onto a road. Turn left onto the road, following it downhill for about 100m. Take the next track off to the right which contours around the moor before leading to a gravel drive about 500m on. Turn right onto this drive and follow it over a steep beck and briefly uphill towards White Wells (9km).

One of the original springs which gave Ilkley its fame as a spa town can be found here. There is also a small museum explaining the history of spas in Ilkley and a cafe where you can linger to enjoy the views before the final descent. Just after the museum there is a steep path that drops down to the left towards the bottom of the moor. Follow this as far as the cattle grid and gate at the bottom and then follow the road down to the junction and traffic lights 500m further down. The main part of town is on your left, the railway station on your right (10km).

Northern Section – Walk Two

Ilkley to Bramhope

Route: Ilkley – Burley Moor – Menston – The Chevin – Bramhope

Distance: 17km; 10.5ml

Time: 4 – 6hr

Ascent: 430m; 1300ft

Maps: 1:25000 Pathfinders: 671 Keighley and Ilkley; 672 Harehills. 1:50000 Landranger: 104 Leeds, Bradford and Harrogate

Getting There

Ilkley is the last stop on the Wharfedale line. Trains run from both Leeds and Bradford (Forster Square). From Leeds trains run half hourly on weekdays and Saturdays, hourly on Sundays. From Bradford they run hourly on weekdays and Saturdays and two hourly on Sundays. There are also buses to Ilkley from Otley and Keighley, as well as Leeds and Bradford.

The Day Ahead

This is an extremely enjoyable walk, which climbs through boulders and craggy faces onto the top of Ilkley Moor before contouring around the edge of the moor for a while. The path drops into the valley, near Burley Woodhead, and follows paths across farmland to Menston which provides a convenient lunchstop. The second half of the walk takes you on a steep climb to the brow of Guiseley Moor, towards the fine woods and downland on top of The Chevin, a justly popular tourist spot. The path continues through the forested eastern end of the Chevin Forest

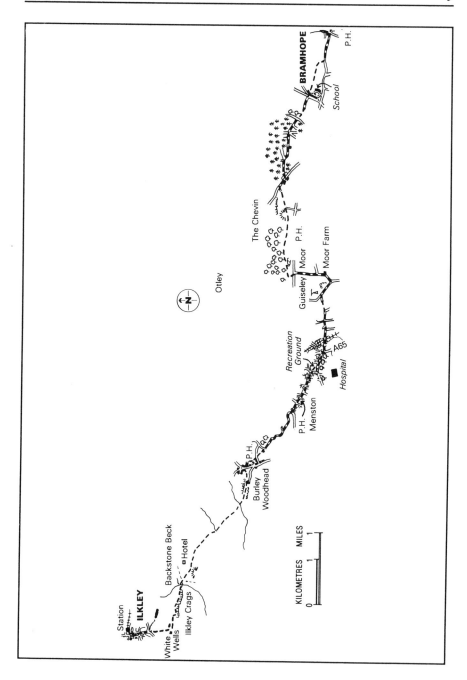

Park before leading to the village of Bramhope.

Menston provides the best option for breaking the walk into two day outings. Trains run from here to Bradford, Leeds and Ilkley (same frequencies as above). Buses from Menston run to Bradford, Harrogate, Leeds and Otley. For details of public transport to and from Bramhope, see the next section.

From Ilkley BR

Turn right out of the station and take the second turning to the left into Wells Promenade. Follow the path and stream up through the wooded island running along the centre of this road. At the top of this short stretch go left, then right and follow the road up towards the moor. Just before the cattle grid bear left and go through the gate ahead. Follow the wide path running straight up the moor towards White Wells, the white buildings ahead. On reaching these buildings turn left and follow the footpath contouring along the side of the moor, for about 300m. After the first large outcrop of boulders take the faint path to the right, leading steeply uphill towards the edge of Ilkley Crags. Reaching the wide footpath at the top turn left and follow this along, keeping close to the crags. After a while this leads into Rocky Valley. This is a short but impressive gully that runs towards the brow of the moor. Emerging from this, the path veers to the left, dropping towards the attractive beck ahead (2km).

Cross the beck and take the path to the right leading to the crest ahead. Once on this top, ignore the broader paths off to the left but turn right going uphill about 50m, before taking another smaller path off to the right. This immediately leads onto the ridge above Hangingstone Road. From here there are wonderful views down the wide expanse of Wharfedale. Follow this ridge which is part of both the Ebor and Dales Ways for about 2km. The footpath here is in good condition, clearly visible, but not too worn.

About half way along this ridge you will pass a row of bright yellow posts stretching up the hillside. These are waymarkers which look strangely out of place on such a barren moor, presumably their brightness makes them more easily seen in mist. Further along the path crosses a small stream and follows a dry stone wall on the left. When the wall ends, head towards the clough ahead – Coldstone Beck. Shortly after crossing this, the paths split; take the one to the left, running downhill along the edge of the clough and passing some rocky outcrops on its descent. Near the bottom of the hill, the path follows a large stone wall round to the right and leaves the moor via a kissing gate, bringing you out to the village of Burley Woodhead (5km).

Turn right onto the road and after 20m turn left down a driveway signposted as the footpath to Menston. At the end of the drive go over a stile on the right, crossing the paddock to a second stile and then onto a gap in the wall at the far end of the next field. Keep to the higher path leading through another gap in the wall and on towards the cottages ahead. Cross the paddock leading to a kissing gate in the corner. Pass through this, cross the drive and go through a second kissing gate onto a fenced path. This path leads to a field where you follow the boundary wall along to the barn ahead. Go through the farm gate next to the barn and continue to the head of the track that ends by the barn. Cross this, picking your way through farm machinery and heading towards the small wood ahead.

The path leads around the edge of the wood, over a small stream and then a stile to a fenced path which brings you out at Bleach Mill. Turn right here and follow this track which leads towards Menston. At the end of the track turn left onto the road and follow this into the centre of the village. Grouped around the first crossroads there are two pubs, The Menston Arms and The Malt Shovel, conveniently at the half way point of the day's walk (7.5km).

Passing through the village, continue straight along the main road for almost 1km until the road bears sharply to the right. Take the footpath to the left which diagonally crosses the green. On joining the main road go left and keep to this for 300m to the junction with the busy A65. Cross this at the traffic lights and turn right. (Harry Ramsden's famous Fish and Chip Restaurant is 1km along this road at the near end of Guiseley). Take the signposted bridleway to the left just after the Fire Station. This is the start of a steep climb to the top of Guiseley Moor and on to The Chevin. Follow the bridleway, crossing a railway line and continuing steeply uphill over a minor road. Carry on climbing for a further 500m to a junction with a second minor road. Looking back from here to Ilkley

Moor and the valley below gives wonderful views and a panorama of most of the day's walking so far (9.5km).

The richly-textured slopes of Ilkley Moor

At the road go right and follow it along for 250m. After passing a quarry on the left hand side, take a track rising to the left, signposted for Moor Farm (10km). Follow this track for nearly 1km to come out on a small road near the top of The Chevin. Turn left onto this road and then almost immediately right following a footpath (signposted) through a hole in the wall to the edge of the woods ahead (11km). Once in the woods, take the path to the right which descends briefly then rises to a dry stone wall. This leads you to the open ridge of The Chevin. This track runs above the woods below and gives wonderful views in both directions along the Wharfe Valley.

This whole area with its mixture of woods, grassland and superb views is a Country Park, and is perhaps the highlight of today's walk. Descending gently along the ridge you pass a large information board.

Continue past this descending along a bridleway towards the East Chevin Road (13km). Take the signposted footpath directly opposite on the other side of the road. Cross the road (with care) and follow this path. After a brief descent it runs uphill, parallel with the road that you have just crossed and emerges at the far end of a small car park. This is one of the major access points for the eastern end of the Chevin Forest Park.

From here take the right hand track, dropping slightly as you approach a clearing and cross over a stream. Shortly after rising away from the stream follow the right hand track (red arrow) which leads towards the edge of the forest. This runs southwards and then turns to the east, passing a trig point on the left hand side (14km). Continue along this track, crossing one junction of paths, before coming to a T-junction of broader tracks. Turn right here and then go left onto a path running next to a dry stone wall. Follow this along, out of the forest and across two fields to a minor road.

The path continues on the opposite side of the road, along a narrow alley and then around the edge of a football pitch and then across a field. At the second stile, veer right and go diagonally across a small field. Then, veer left and follow the dry stone wall along to a broader path which leads out to a road (16km). Turn left at the road and follow it to the Village Cross in the centre of Bramhope. Most of the village amenities are grouped around the cross, with a pub, a baker and newsagent within a few metres of one another. To pick up the public transport routes to Leeds and Otley, turn left at the cross and drop to the junction below (17km). Buses to Leeds stop on the opposite side of the road, to Otley just in front of the church.

Northern Section – Walk Three

Bramhope to Wetherby

Route: Bramhope – Bank Top – Stank – Harewood – Woodhall – Linton – Wetherby

Distance: 24km; 15ml

Time: 6 – 8hr

Ascent: 300m; 1000ft

Maps: 1.25000 Pathfinders: 672 Harehills and 673 Tadcaster; 1:50000 Landrangers: 104 Leeds, Bradford and Harrogate; 105 York.

Getting There

This area, to the north east of Leeds, is in the middle of the largest gap on the Metro rail network. There are no train connections to either the start or the finish of this walk, so buses need to be used at both ends. Buses to Bramhope (numbers 780/ 782/ 783/ 784) run three times an hour from the Headrow in Leeds during the week, but only hourly on Sundays and Bank Holidays. For details of bus services from Wetherby see the next chapter.

In view of Wetherby being some distance from the towns in the west of the county, some people may find it a more attractive idea to link this walk with the next one to make a weekend outing. Bed and breakfast accommodation is available in Wetherby and there is also an official camping site near the racecourse, 2km outside the town.

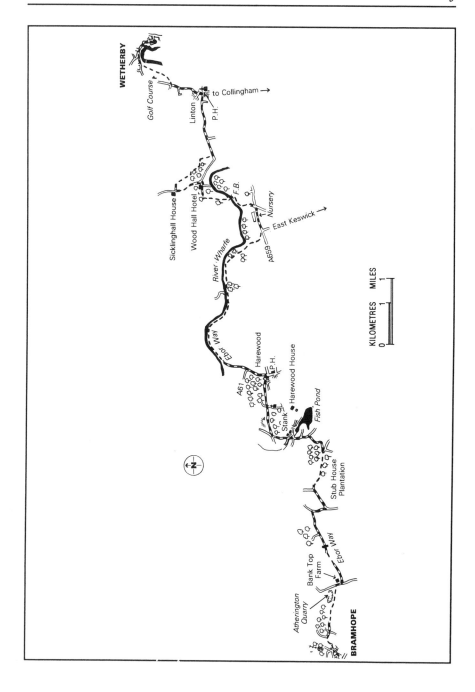

The Day Ahead

This section is longer than the two previous ones and although it doesn't reach such heights as the earlier days it does involve a thousand feet of ascent. The route closely follows the Ebor Way for most of the day as it runs east along Wharfedale. For the first half of the day, it stays on the ridge above Wharfedale as far as Harewood, from where the path drops and follows the riverbank for several miles. The last part of the walk is spent to the north of the Wharfe, on the farmland, parkland and minor roads that lead to Wetherby.

After leaving Bramhope the only shops and pub that the route passes for the next 20km are at Harewood, some half way along the route. The food at the Harewood Arms is highly recommended by several guides, although a full three-course meal may slow your pace down in the afternoon. For those who wish to do the walk in two shorter sections, Harewood is also the best place to stop, offering the attraction of the stately home with its extensive gardens. There are regular half hourly bus services between Leeds and Harrogate that stop here. The other points where the walk crosses bus routes are on the A659 near East Keswick and at Linton. Details for these routes are the same as for Wetherby buses and are given at the start of the next chapter. There is a wide range of restaurants, cafes and pubs in Wetherby.

From Bramhope Church

Take the bridleway on the opposite side of the road from the church. Follow this down for about 300m, between gardens and the grounds of a hotel on the left-hand side, before emerging onto a suburban road. Turn right onto the road and, after 50m, take the path between the houses on the left (signposted as a bridleway). The bridleway comes to another residential street where it continues along the edge of the drive of the house immediately opposite. The bridleway continues to descend between the houses for a further 150m, before coming out on another residential road. Again, the bridleway goes along the edge of the driveway of the house immediately opposite. From here it starts to leave the houses behind and drops towards a small beck before rising to meet a minor road (1km).

Turn right onto this road, following it round one bend and onto a second bend with a bridge just beyond it. Turn left just before the bridge onto a signposted bridleway running due east. Keep straight along this bridleway for just over 1km, ignoring the track turning off to the right. Near the end of this stretch the path runs close to a large quarry, with magnificent cliffs exposed to the south. There is a sizeable population of crows around, who have clearly thrive in this environment. At the end of the path turn right onto the road, rising gently uphill before taking the bridleway on the left, signposted for Bank Top (3km).

From here, the walking becomes easy as you follow this lane for 2km, rising slowly at first and then dropping quite sharply. The views over the Wharfe are good, though not as spectacular as those enjoyed the previous day. Eventually this track joins a minor road where you go right, steeply uphill for about 200m. At the T-junction at the top go left dropping for about 400m to where the road veers sharply to the left. From here take the signposted bridleway to the right leading towards the forest ahead. This is Stub House Plantation, the western edge of a large belt of deciduous woodlands that run south and west from the Harewood Estate.

Follow the track through these woods, taking the lower route to the left when the tracks diverge. After descending through the woodland, which is rich with wildfowl, the path emerges at the edge of some parkland, with a large lake visible to the right. A little to the left of the lake, Harewood House can be seen on the southern flanks of the hill ahead. The path skirts around the edge of the parkland, leading to the edge of the walled estate. Go left here and climb a small rise which then drops into the unfortunately named hamlet of Stank (7.5km). This is the working part of the Harewood Estate and has no public facilities.

Follow the signposted bridleway uphill out of the hamlet, and at the top of the hill follow the track round to the right. This leads to a long straight drive which, after 1.5km, comes out at the village of Harewood. About halfway along this route, there is a track off to the right that leads to a remote church in a forest clearing, well worth visiting. Arriving on the busy A61 in Harewood, the route turns left. About 100m on the right is the only inn before approaching Wetherby. At almost the halfway point of today's walk, it makes a very welcome stopping off point (9.5km)

Farmbuildings at Stank

Follow the A61 northwards dropping steeply downhill for about 300m. At the sharp left-hand bend in the road take the signposted track (Ebor Way) that runs straight ahead (10km). Follow this all the way down to the River Wharfe turning right at the bottom to follow the river downstream for about 3.5km. This is a peaceful and flat stretch of walking, where the only company is likely to be that of a few fishermen. No navigational problems here, though there is one section of woodland with irritatingly high undergrowth. On my last visit here I was privileged to see the blue flash of a kingfisher on the far bank, and a host of dragonflies.

After the second stretch of woodland, the path climbs up a bank and crosses a stile before climbing away from the river. This path emerges on another fast road the A659, which you follow to the left for about 400m. At the first road junction (coming in from the right) take the signposted track to the left. (Buses from Wetherby to Leeds stop on this corner). The path provides an easy and quick descent back to the riverbank. Once the path flattens, Woodhall Bridge appears ahead. Take the right-hand path to reach it (16km).

Once on the opposite bank the path rises gently at first, then more steeply towards some woods. At the edge of these woods, follow the bridleway to the right. This crosses the drives of several exclusive residences, before passing between the Woodhall Hotel (on the right) and a monastery (on the left). Just after the monastery the bridleway turns left into some woods, signposted for Sicklinghall. Follow this for almost 1km to the first set of buildings, Sicklinghall House. Just after these buildings, and before the road begins, turn right around the north edge of a field and then right again towards the edge of Lime Kiln Wood. Follow the path through the wood, and then around its perimeter for about 500m. The path turns left for less than 100m, then right again through a further small patch of woods to reach a surfaced bridleway (19.5km).

Turn left onto this and follow it for more 2km to the village of Linton. Once in Linton, turn left and follow the road towards Wetherby, keeping to the right at the first junction. This approach road to Wetherby is lined by exclusive residences with lengthy drives. About 1km along this road, just 100m after the bus stop on the left, take the path through the hedge on the right, signposted (although not very clearly). This runs NNE across the golf course, crossing an old railway embankment and then through fields and over a recreation ground before emerging on the road just outside the centre of Wetherby. Turn right onto the road and follow it through to the town centre.

The centre of Wetherby is delightful, with interesting architecture spanning many centuries. Particularly interesting are The Shambles, The Weir and the streets around the church. There is a wide choice of eating establishments, including a usually packed fish and chip shop next to the main bus stops and a wide selection of hostelries to slake your thirst.

Eastern Section – Walk One

Wetherby to East Garforth

Route: Wetherby – Thorp Arch – Boston Spa – Bramham – Bramham Park – Becca Park – Aberford – Parlington Hollins – East Garforth

Distance: 26km; 16ml

Time: 7 – 9 hr

Ascent: 285m; 940ft

Maps: 1:25000 Pathfinders: 673 Tadcaster; 684 Garforth. 1:50000 Landranger: 105 York

Getting There

Wetherby is a 50 minute bus ride to the north east of Leeds. Services (numbers 794 – 799) run half hourly on weekdays and Saturdays, hourly on Sundays. They depart from Infirmary Street, Leeds, which is just behind the main Post Office on City Square, two minutes walk from the train station. There are also bus services to Wetherby from Harrogate, Knaresborough and York. For details of public transport from East Garforth see the following chapter.

The Day Ahead

At 16 miles, this is the longest day on the West Yorkshire Way. It is mostly flat, and has long stretches of straight paths and bridleways making for easy walking and navigation. It is possible to break this walk into smaller sections, the logically stopping points being at Bramham (11km) and/or Aberford (20km). The 741 bus service between Leeds and Wetherby passes through Bramham, offering a link in either direction.

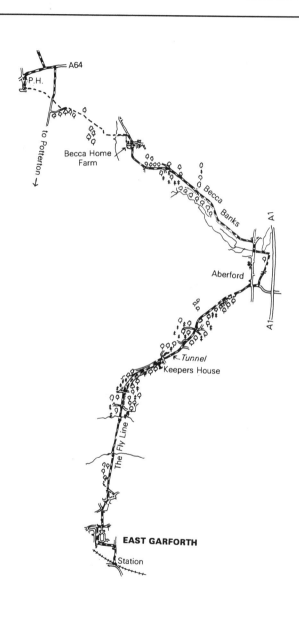

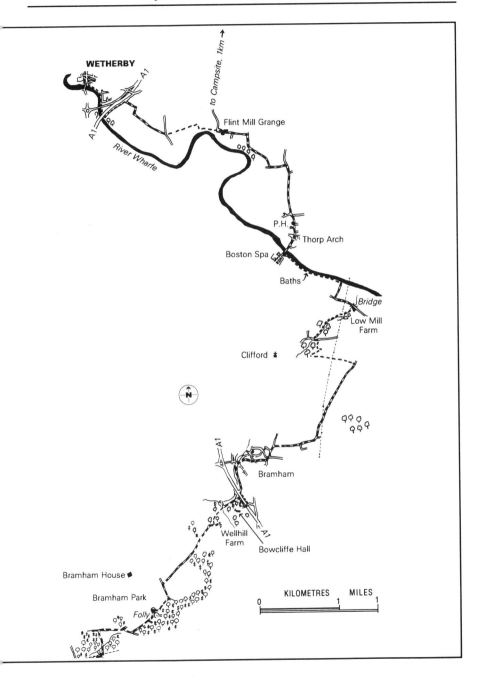

The 64 service from Leeds terminates at Aberford. There is also an irregular bus service, the 478, that almost shadows the route of the walk, linking Thorp Arch, Boston Spa, Bramham, Aberford and Garforth. There are several pubs in every village that the walk passes through, although shops and cafes are thin on the ground. A packed lunch or some other foodstuffs are therefore strongly recommended.

The day begins in Wetherby, the bridging point over the River Wharfe for the A1. Nowadays, the Great North Road bypasses the town which, in large part, it helped to create as a market town. The walk links with the Ebor Way, 1km outside the town, and follows this over rolling countryside, through Thorp Arch to Boston Spa. Here the West Yorkshire Way leaves the Ebor way behind and follows several of the paths that form "Day Walks in the Limestone Country". These paths lead around the edge of Clifford, and through the pretty villages of Bramham and Aberford. The walk also includes long sections through two large and well maintained estates, Bramham Park and the Parlington Estate. For those who like rolling countryside and shady woods, this is an ideal day's outing.

From Wetherby High Street

The bus will drop you near the bottom of the High Street. Cross the road, turn left and follow it for 50m towards the bridge. Just before the junction turn right onto Weir Garth, the stairway that leads towards the river which passes the town's spectacular weir. Once onto the river bank turn left and follow the path under the bridge. As you pass under this gracious bridge you will notice that it has been built over the remains of an earlier one, whose arches are still visible. Continue along the path, which leads into a car park, and then beyond past a popular picnic site. Follow the path as it runs close to the river bank for about 500m, passing some chalk banks on the left. The path then goes under two road bridges, the second of which carries the A1. After the second bridge turn left onto a track that climbs and then runs parallel with the A1 for a short distance. Follow this towards the first gate (1km).

The Ebor Way is signposted straight on here, but that will lead you straight back to Wetherby. Instead, once through the gate go right and cross a stile into a green lane, bordered by high hedges. Follow this along for about 200m and at the first junction of tracks go right again.

The Wharfe at Wetherby

Follow this for a further 100m and, at the next junction, go left. After a few metres this leads to a drive, flanked by telegraph poles. Go straight along this drive to the metalled road, 500m ahead (2km). Cross the road and follow the path towards some woods ahead. On reaching the woods keep them to your right, and the path shortly emerges at Flint Mill Grange (3km).

Go straight through the farm yard and then straight on, towards Flint Mill. The track becomes a road for 100m before the road turns off to the house on the right. The broad footpath continues straight ahead to the junction, 200m further on, where you turn right and follow the track towards some woods. At the edge of the woods, the path turns left and follows the edge of the woodland for 300m before leaving the woods behind and crossing another open field. At the next junction of tracks turn left and, after a further 200m, you reach a road. Turn right here and follow the road to Thorp Arch (5km)

This is a picturesque garden village, with some fine architecture, including Georgian houses. The road takes you straight through the village, to the narrow road bridge leading to Boston Spa. After the first house on the other side of the bridge, take the footpath to the left (signposted 'riverside walk'). Follow this along the banks of the Wharfe for 1km, passing the original (and surprisingly small) Spa Houses half way along this section (6km). 500m further on, there is a small path to the right leading away from the river bank. Here you leave the Ebor Way for the last time and follow the path between gardens to a road. Turn left onto the road and cross it, passing some well kept allotments on the right, a line of pylons and a small bridge over a beck. At the far side of the bridge, just beyond the white railings, turn right into the yard of Low Mill Farm (7km).

The footpath runs through the farm yard and then out of the back of the yard, passing a pond before turning right to climb a short bank. At the top of the bank go left and follow the edge of the wood and the course of the beck below. This path leads over four stiles to the next road. While crossing these fields you may notice an unusual church on the skyline to the right. This is the Catholic church at Clifford, the design of which is reputedly based on Angouleme Cathedral in central France. The catholic community at Clifford successfully sought the support of European nobility and aristocracy to help raise the funds for the church.

Once onto the road go left across a bridge and, after 50m, take the signposted footpath to the right. This leads by some woods before turning left towards a stile. Cross the stile and follow the path running straight ahead, keeping the fence to your right-hand side. Here there are even finer views of the church, and the line of the nave and the silhouette of the rose window at its eastern end can be clearly distinguished. After 200m, along this path you arrive at another stile (8km).

Cross this and follow the path to the left, leading away from Clifford. This broad flat path marks the start of a period of easy navigation. Keep to this path for 750m, passing under some pylons, before reaching a minor road. Turn right here and follow the road for 2km to the edge of Bramham. Along the way you pass under the same line of pylons as before and shortly before Bramham the road swings to the right. Arriving at a T-junction, go left and follow the road to the next junction. Turn right here and very soon after take the second right into High Street. This leads into the centre of the village, dropping down a bank to bring you to the village square (11km).

Bramham is another attractive and peaceful limestone country village, whose skyline is accentuated by the contours of the land. While it boasts three pubs, it has only one shop and a garage. From the village cross in Bramham, turn left, following the sign for the A1 (South). Follow this road for about 500m, then take the pavement running off to the left which swings to the right, leading to the edge of the A1. Don't even think about crossing the road here, but follow the footpath to the left leading up a bank to a bridge over the road. Cross the bridge, and turn right on the other side, coming back down the bank. At the bottom of the bank turn left along the drive (signposted 'footpath') passing a sign announcing the entrance to Bramham Park. Follow the paths through the woods for about 700m. At the first fork, in a clearing of the woods, keep to the left rising steeply up a bank towards Wellhill Farm (12.5km). At the top of the bank the drive swings to the left again, go right here following the arrows into the woods. Follow the path through the woods and the gate beyond to come out onto a broad track running across open farmland. Follow this path for 1km to a junction of paths where a prominent sign points you to the left (13.5km).

Folly in Bramham Park

Continue towards the woods ahead and just before the white gates turn
right along the well-signed path that leads along the edge of the woods.
This runs south-westwards for about 1km. About halfway along its
length, it skirts around a curious circular, colonnaded building (14km).
This is marked as a temple on the map, and is part of the elaborate
gardens of Bramham Park, which has been described as "The Versailles
of Yorkshire". Behind the temple, a high obelisk can be seen. Half a
kilometre past these monuments, the path leads into a stretch of
woodland.

Once in the woods, follow the signposted track to the right, dropping
slightly before the track turns to the left. Quite soon the woods on the
right give way to open fields, then after a short while those on the left
do the same. Soon a conifer plantation appears on the left. Turn left and
take the path along the edge of this which, after 300m, runs into the
woods. At the corner of the wood turn right and follow the path running
parallel to the pylons. After 200m this leads to a dirt track (which is the
highest point on today's walk at 300ft above sea level). Go left here to
come out near Kiddal Lane-End (16km).

Beware of this road! It is the main Leeds – York trunk road (A64) and the traffic moves very fast. Turn left and follow the road along, crossing when it is safe to do so. After 100m, go right onto a minor road signposted for Potterton and Barwick. After 400m, take the footpath signposted off to the left, through a gap in the hedge. Follow this path diagonally across the field towards the woods on the right. Cross the stile in the corner of the field and continue along by the wood for 500m.

At the corner of the second field the path cuts into the woods for a short while before coming out at a stile. After the stile carry straight on, keeping the fence to your right, until you reach another stile. Carry straight on to some farm gates. Go through these and follow the line of trees and bushes on your right-hand side until they peter out. At this point head for the large yellow board on the solitary tree ahead at 11 o' clock. From here, look for a similar marker just to the left of a small line of thorn bushes. From these look for the third yellow marker that leads to the track to your left. Go right onto the track and follow it to Becca Home Farm (17.5km).

At the farm go straight across the junction of tracks following the track running due south between the farm buildings. This soon gives way to a path which veers left and then leads to the corner of some woods. Go through the gate beyond the woods and cross the parkland. After 200m this leads to the edge of some more woods. Keep straight on with the woods to your right. Ignore the first footpath sign to the right but, 20m further on, turn right onto a dirt track. This leads to the top of Becca Banks, a series of iron age earthworks and then straight on for 1.5km to the village of Aberford (20km).

Aberford is a pretty village strung out along the crossing of Cock Beck. The A1 used to run right through the centre of the village, but has now been diverted to the east, enabling the village to retrieve much of its tranquillity. Like Bramham it appears blessed with more pubs than shops and, similarly, appears popular with commuters from Leeds. At the road junction in Aberford turn right onto the main road. Cross the road and take the footpath that runs parallel with the main road. This leads over a wooden footbridge; once over this, turn left along the small road which soon becomes a footpath. This takes you over three stiles and leads up a bank, to within earshot of the A1. Nearing the top of the bank follow the dry stone wall to the right to a stile which leads into a paddock. Keep to the bottom of this field heading towards another stile and gate. Once over the stile follow the drive past some gardens to the road beyond where you turn right (21km).

100m further on there is a T-junction; cross the road ahead and follow the signposted footpath on the opposite side of the road along Parlington Lane. Follow this bridleway which runs for 2km through the Parlington Estate, keeping to the right at the only fork along this stretch. This track is the route of an old railway line, built to carry coal from the pits at Garforth to a distribution point at Aberford. Along this track you pass under two tunnels, one quite short. The second and longer tunnel, is lit by natural skylights in the roof. The railway line didn't pass through this tunnel, but to the south of it. This tunnel was a landscaping exercise, built to screen the train line from the now demolished big house on the estate. Shortly after this second tunnel this track leads to the Gamekeeper's House (23km).

Immediately after the Keeper's house, take the signposted footpath, running off to the left. This path, known as The Flyline, runs all the way to Garforth. A few years ago, the local council took a case all the way to the Crown Courts to keep this path open when it was faced with an attempted closure. Good for them, as it is a lovely path, running through extensive woodland and providing a useful link for locals and visitors alike. Keep straight along this path for 1km through the woodland, crossing two junctions of paths. Emerging from the woodland, the track continues due south for a further 1.5km, passing the site of some of the early pits, to the junction with the road in Garforth (25.5km).

Cross the road and turn right. After the bus stop, take the signposted footpath to the left which runs between the houses. Follow this to where a road comes in from the left and go left along this, into the housing estate on your right. Continue to the end of the road and turn right into Meadow Lane. Soon this turns into a footpath running across open ground. There are disused mine shafts marked on the map close to this path: evidence that you are now on the edge of the Yorkshire Coal Seams. Continue along this path, as it winds round to the left, leading to the bright red bridge that marks the train station at East Garforth (26km). Trains for Leeds, Bradford and Halifax depart from the opposite platform.

Eastern Section – Walk Two

East Garforth to Knottingley

Route: East Garforth -Kippax – Ledston Luck – Ledsham – Fairburn Ings – Brotherton – Ferrybridge – Knottingley

Distance: 17km; 10.5ml

Time: 4 – 6 hr

Ascent: 150m; 465ft

Maps: 1:25000 Pathfinders 684 Garforth; 693 Castleford and Pontefract. 1:50000 Landranger: 105 York

Getting There

East Garforth is the last station but one, within the Metro area on the main Leeds to York line. Trains run half hourly from Leeds (also stopping at Bradford and Halifax beforehand) on Mondays to Saturdays and hourly on Sundays. For train connections from Knottingley see the next chapter.

The Day Ahead

This is one of the shorter stages of the walk, running around the edges of well-drained limestone soils and the South Yorkshire coal seams. The gently rolling hills around this area offer pleasant and constantly changing views. Starting around the recently expanded settlements of East Garforth and Kippax, the walk soon leads into rolling countryside. It passes through much woodland, nearly all of which is an interesting mix of deciduous species.

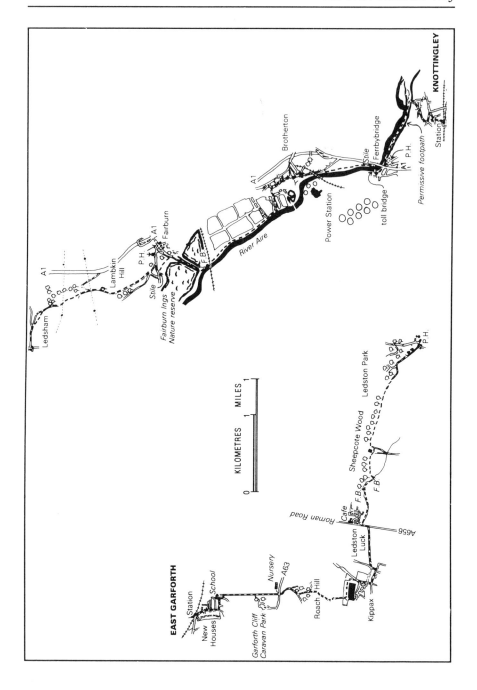

The walk also takes in Fairburn Ings, probably the most important bird reserve in the county. These artificial lakes are part of the legacy of the coal mining industry which was once so important a part of the economy around Castleford. The last seven kilometres closely follow the Aire downstream. The huge power station at Ferrybridge dominates the skyline for much of this stretch until the final section beyond Ferrybridge, which runs along a recently restored path between canal and river. This leads towards the centre of Knottingley, traditionally a centre of the glass industry.

The route is well-endowed with services, with a cafe on the new industrial park at Ledston Luck, and Public Houses in Ledsham, Fairburn, Brotherton, Ferrybridge and Knottingley. Few of these are open in the afternoon so, if you are starting late, go prepared with your own refreshments. For breaking the walk into shorter sections there are several options. From Ledston Luck there is a bus service (160) that runs between Castleford and Leeds. From Ledsham, the half way point of the walk, there is a 2 hourly bus service (175) between East Garforth and Castleford. The 492 can be picked up at Brotherton to take you to Pontefract (occasionally this service extends in the opposite direction as far as Tadcaster). Finally from Ferrybridge there are many bus links to Knottingley, Castleford, Wakefield and Leeds.

From East Garforth BR

Cross the bridge over the railway line (if coming from the Leeds direction). Turn right into Woodlands Drive and then left at the T-junction immediately ahead. Continue along this suburban street for several hundred metres. Take the fifth turning to the left – Ribblesdale Avenue; don't worry if you lose count, as this turning is on the corner of the first bend of the road. This quickly leads to a school, where the road turns sharply to the right. About 50m further on, turn left and then right onto a signposted footpath that runs due south for 1km. Near the end of this path cross the tracks of a miniature railway, and continue along the broad drive and across a car park to the A63 (1.5km).

Cross the road with care and continue along the signposted footpath directly opposite which leads to some woods. Pass through one kissing gate and then at a second gate follow the arrows to the left. This path follows a fence gently uphill, leading to a stile. Cross the stile and continue to the crest of Roach Hill (2km). From here there are good views across Kippax, with the church tower at the top of the town just visible above the treeline. On a clear day the views go beyond Kippax to the Pennine foothills.follow the footpath between two fences to a gap, then continue to descend more steeply to the right. Follow the path as it veers round to the left towards some scrub wood below. When the paths fork keep to the right and follow this towards the houses at the edge of Kippax (2.5km).

Go through the gap by the "no tipping sign", into the cul-de-sac beyond. Go right here, left 20m further on and then left again into Sandgate Drive. Follow this uphill for about 300m, past the first road off to the right and, a few metres beyond this, go right along a path between the houses. Follow this footpath to a T-junction 200m downhill. Turn left onto the main road and go uphill for about 400m, passing a set of well kept allotments on your left. Nearing the top of the hill, take the first road to the left, Sandgate Terrace.

Follow this along for 200m and then take the gravel track off to the left. Less than 100m along this go right onto a tarmac footpath that leads into open countryside. From here you can see the towers of Ferrybridge Power Station which will provide a landmark throughout much of the days walk. Continue along this path to the A656, an old Roman Road. Turn left onto the road and after 100m turn right following the signposted footpath away from the village (4.5km). (A couple of hundred metres up the road you can find the village of Ledston Luck, with its new enterprise park and attendant cafe).

From here the path to Ledsham is straightforward. Leaving the road it runs along the edge of the village, and then continues following the line of a drainage ditch and a wood. After about 1km, the woodland curves around to the left and the drainage ditch runs off to the right. Cross the footbridge and continue following the path along the edge of the wood. After a further 0.5km this leads to Sheepcote Farm. Cross the stile before the farm and follow the signposted footpath that keeps you to the right of the farm buildings. Cross a second stile and a track to come out onto another track. This looks like a practice racecourse, with a rail on the far side and sand underfoot.

The old church at Ledsham

Turn left onto this track, and follow it round to the edge of another strip of woodland. Keep to the well defined path running alongside the woodland for a further 1km. Eventually the path leads onto a broader track, which leads into the woods (7km). Soon this track becomes an unsurfaced road, passing a farm and several cottages. This leads out to the village of Ledsham. The first building you see as you approach the village centre is the Chequers Inn, a convenient and pleasant place to mark the half way point of the day's walk (8km).

From the inn go along the main road, Claypit Lane, passing the medieval church on your left. Follow the road around a tight turn; the footpath is separated from the road here for good reason as this corner is blind and can be very dangerous! The road soon takes you beyond the end of the village. When it veers sharply left, turn off to the right through a kissing gate, next to a five-bar gate. The footpath veers to the right of the broad track that runs up the bank to cross open pasture for 0.5km before leading to a wood. Keep this to your left-hand side, crossing a clearing in the wood after a few hundred metres.

Pass under some pylons half way across this clearing and aim for the small finger of woodland immediately ahead (9km). Cross the stile into the wood and after 100m cross another stile leading back out of the wood. You are now in North Yorkshire. Carry on straight ahead to where a line of bushes runs down the bank. Keep to the left of these and follow the faint path to the top of Lambkin Hill. Follow the boundary fence along the top of the hill for 1km, at one point crossing a stile to put the boundary fence on your right-hand side. From the top of this hill you can catch inspiring views of Fairburn Ings and the towns of Castleford and Pontefract beyond.

Keeping to the top of the bank, you come to a stile leading to a track that passes between a house on your right and a small wood on the left (10km). Follow this to the minor road below, and turn right before taking the footpath 300m downhill on the left. This narrow path wends its way between houses for 100m or so, before crossing a stile and leading across rough pastureland towards the causeway ahead. On reaching the broad track go over the stile, turn right and follow the sandy causeway that runs between two large artificial lakes. These are sites of industrial dereliction having been created by mining subsidence. They are also now Sites of Special Scientific Interest (SSSIs in "ecospeak"), attracting many birds, the species changing with the passing of the seasons.

Even if (like the author) you don't know a tern from a ringneck, you can still enjoy the many different sorts of birds and soak in the undisturbed nature of this reserve, reputedly one of the finest in Yorkshire. You don't have to be a "twitcher" to appreciate that this is a very special place. At the end of the causeway there is the opportunity for a brief detour off to the right to explore more of the reserve. The path between the river and the lakes is elevated and affords great views of the largest lake and its attendant birdlife. There are also hides along here for periods of sustained lake watching. Birders are a rather silent lot, for obvious reasons, so respect this by passing quietly.

To continue along the route, turn left away from the Causeway and follow the Aire downstream towards the power station. Cross a pair of sluice gates and under a railway bridge (11.5km). Follow the riverbank for 1.5km, drawing ever closer to the power station. This provides a source of fascination, with the comings and goings of the trains and flat barges bringing coal to the power station and rumblings from within the buildings. Drawing ever closer to the power station, you reach a large pair of gates across the path. Turn left, away from the river, and follow the footpath between two high chain link fences. These guard large pools, one now reclaimed and full of reeds and sometimes birdlife, the other impenetrably murky. When these fences end carry straight on across a junction of tracks, follow the path up towards the houses marking the edge of Brotherton ahead (11km).

At this junction you may notice a large pair of blue gates on your right with the letters EMGB across them. These are the initials of the East Midlands Generating Board, now some 40 years defunct. Back along the river you may have noticed gates or signs with the initials CEGB (Central Electricity Generating Board). This was the successor of the Regional Generating Boards. If you look at the main entrance to the power station later, you will see the new board bears the legend National Power. How long will it be before the electricity industry is further reorganised and another name board appears?

Follow the path up to the road and turn right following the road to the T-junction. Turn right again and follow the road to the left, passing the Church of Edward the Confessor on the right and then under a railway bridge. The village of Brotherton provides unusual contrasts between the country cottages on one side and the industrial scenery on the far bank of the river. Opposite the last houses in the village there is a signposted footpath leading back towards the river bank (14km). Follow this towards the prominent concrete bridge ahead. This carries the new dual lane A1 over the river. In its shadow is a far older bridge that predates the motor car and which will carry you over to Ferrybridge.

To get onto the bridge, look for the stile in the fence on the left about 100m before the bridge itself. From here the path is clearly defined. Unfortunately this fine bridge is suffering from the abuses of the modern times, both from graffiti sprayers and the theft of many of its paving stones.

Once over the bridge, the pavement goes to the left, passing the Old Toll House on your right. Follow the road round and pass under the A1 bridge (15km). Turn left onto the signposted canal walk just before the Golden Lion. Here the Calder and Aire Navigation separates from the River Aire. Cross the canal by the high white bridge and turn right onto the sliver of land that separates the two waterways. This land has been restored by Wakefield Groundwork Trust and makes for a very pleasant towpath walk along this permissive right of way. After crossing a small bridge after 100m the path continues along the towpath for a further 1km taking you around the back of Knottingley.

The Old Toll House at Ferrybridge

Approaching a large butter-coloured factory (King's Mill), pass through a kissing gate and take the footbridge over the canal. Continue up to the road and turn right. Almost immediately after, when the road veers to the right, take the second left up Holes Lane (signposted as a 'no through road'). Follow this along, noting the simple yet well planned bungalows on the right-hand side. Follow Holes Lane along to the junction with the main road. Turn left and then right at the traffic lights ahead. The first turning on the left leads to the railway station (17km).

Eastern Section – Walk Three

Knottingley to South Elmsall

Route: Knottingley – Womersley Park – Little Smeaton – Wentbridge – Thorpe Audlin – Upton – South Elmsall

Distance: 23.5km; 15ml

Ascent: 180m; 625ft

Time: 5 – 7 hours

Maps: 1:25000 Pathfinders 693 Castleford and Pontefract; 704 Hemsworth and Askern. 1:50000 Landranger: 111 Sheffield and Doncaster

Getting There

There is an hourly train service to Knottingley from both Wakefield and Leeds on Mondays to Saturdays. On Sundays trains only run from Leeds and are two hourly. There are also direct buses to Knottingley from Leeds, Wakefield, Pontefract and Castleford. Returning from the end of the walk there is a choice of railway stations to use. South Elmsall is the closer of the two; Moorthorpe is a further 1.5km along the route of the West Yorkshire Way. Both stations will take you back to Wakefield and Leeds. For details of connections to both stations see the following chapter.

The day ahead

This is a pleasant day's walk along the byways and footpaths of this little visited corner of the county. There is a considerable amount of road walking today, but they are nearly all quiet country lanes. The walk strays into North Yorkshire for a seven-mile stretch between Stubbs Lane and Wentbridge, passing through the villages at Smeaton and the picturesque nature reserve at Brockadale before coming back into West Yorkshire at Wentbridge.

This is the most easterly section of the West Yorkshire Way and also the flattest. Looking eastwards on the map from Knottingley there is hardly a contour line to be seen. This is the edge of the flat lands that run from here to the Humber Estuary. Part of today's walk also falls within the Yorkshire coal fields and much of the landscape has been shaped by the mining industry. In recent years, of course, that industry has been cut back enormously and there are no more working pits in this area. However in some places, the scars of the mining industry remain. In others reclamation projects are creating new landscapes. What does remain are the power stations of the M62 "Energy Belt", built to run on local coal. At one point during the walk, you can see three different power stations from the same vantage point.

The best opportunities for refreshments and for breaking the walk into two parts are at the Smeatons. Little Smeaton is approximately half way along the route and has a friendly pub. From Kirk Smeaton there is an hourly bus service (412) to Pontefract. Wentbridge is on the same bus route and also has an inn. There are several buses from Upton, mostly running towards Barnsley. The 84, 85, 246, 247, and 249 services all go to South Elmsall; the 249 also runs to Pontefract and the 485 on to Wakefield. At the end of the walk South Elmsall and Moorthorpe have a wide selection of pubs and takeaways, including pubs next to each station.

Starting Point – Knottingley BR

Take the drive out of the railway station up to the main road. Turn right onto this road and go right again at the traffic lights onto Headland Lane. Cross the bridge over the railway line and go left at the junction of the roads beyond. Follow the road across two sets of railway tracks, and after these take the first road to the right into The Ridgeway (1km). Follow the road through the estate and round as it swings to the left 400m further on. Turn right at the T-junction ahead and follow this road, which deteriorates into a track and leads to a tunnel under the railway line. Cross under the railway line and carry straight on for 1km, ignoring the path off to the right after 100m or so. Continue along this track to

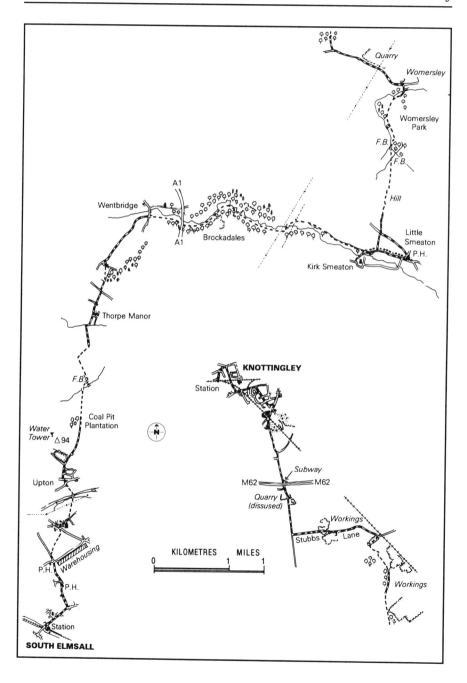

another tunnel runs under the M62 (3km).

Keep straight along this track, passing a disused quarry on the right. At the road junction, almost 1km from the subway, turn left and follow Stubbs Lane for 1.5km as far as a railway crossing (5.5km). Immediately before the crossing, take the signposted bridleway that runs between two chain link fences. Follow this for almost 2km. After a while the fence on the right drops away and the path continues to run close to the fence on the left. This track leads past mineworkings, woodland and open farmland. As you progress along this path, the harsher aspects of the landscape disappear and the woods become more dominant. After a brief descent out of the woods the track runs along the side of one field and emerges onto a road (7.5km).

Turn left here and follow the road for 1.5km to the edge of Womersley. Just before the first house in the village on the right-hand side, go over a stone stile on the right. Follow the signposted footpath down the bank and over the brook below (9km). Once over this, follow the path as it runs close to the fence on the left and after 300m leads to a stile at the edge of some woodland. Follow the path along the edge of the woods for 400m, until a discreet sign points you onto a path into the woods on the right. This path soon brings you out on the far side of the woods at the edge of a drainage ditch. Follow this ditch along to the left for 200m and then cross it at the wooden footbridge (10km).

Once over the ditch go left and follow the path into another field. Cut across the edge of this field to a gap in the hedge opposite. (This is about 100m up from the woods to your left). There is another small footbridge on the other side of this gap. Cross this and head to the right towards the hedgerow above. The path crosses this hedgerow and runs uphill across the field above. At the top of this field the path becomes a wide track running uphill, slightly to the right of the brow of the hill. Continue over the top of the hill and down to a road junction. A sign points to the left offering you a detour to a conveniently located pub, The Fox, 400m to the east in Little Smeaton.

The route itself continues straight over this junction, leading downhill to a T-junction 400m below. Go right here, turning into Hodge Lane (11.5km). To rejoin the footpath from the pub, a stroll along the main (and only) street of Little Smeaton, leads to the same junction, where you will continue straight on. Once into Hodge Lane there is a splendid view across the valley to Kirk Smeaton. Keep to the top road, ignoring the road dropping off to the left by the red telephone kiosk. The road soon turns into a drive and then to a footpath which leads along the edge of a field. Keep to the top of the ridge for 1km. The woodland gives way to open views and then the path returns to a strip of woodland. At the end of this, just after the first set of pylons, the path begins to drop to the left, crossing a lower field, and then on to a grassy bank and through a hedge to lead to a white footbridge (13km).

Kirk Smeaton

Cross the river here and then take the path to the left. This runs parallel with the river for a few metres and then continues to the bottom of the steep bank ahead. Turn right and follow the line of trees to a metal stile. Once over this you are in the thick woodland of the Brockadale nature reserve. The path follows the meanderings of Brockadale for 1.5km before emerging into clearer meadows under the imposing sweep of the Wentbridge Viaduct (15km).

Passing under the viaduct, continue along the same path, rising slightly to approach the village of Wentbridge. There is an interesting chapel perched on the opposite side of the valley on the approach to the village. The village itself is charming, although very small. Once onto the road in the village, cross over and take the road directly opposite, signposted for Thorpe Audlin. This road leads into open country and for most of its length has a pavement alongside it. After Ikm, nearing the top of a rise, a couple of bungalows appear on the left. Take the path through the gate on the left, just before them and follow the edge of the field around for about 30m to a gap in the hedge. Go right through this gap between the gardens, which is quite overgrown, to the drive and stone stile (17km).

Cross the stile and follow the footpath over another stile and along the well-marked footpath to the bottom corner of the woods on the left. Here the path veers to the right a little and follows a hedge along the edge of a field to the road ahead. Turn left at the road and then right onto the minor road signposted for Thorpe Manor. At the next crossroads carry straight on down Causeway Garth Lane towards the old village. Some 200m through the village the tarmac drive turns to the left, carry straight on along the gravel drive leading to a drainage ditch (18km). The track swings to the right after the ditch, heading towards a house. Go left at the gate, taking the broad track that rises slightly and then peters out after 300m. Go right here climbing slightly to the bank ahead. At the solitary tree near the top go left and follow the path down for 0.5km to the footbridge at the bottom (19km).

Go right, over the footbridge and follow the path along the edge of the ditch to the second of two footbridges on your left. The path rises from here, leading to the wood above. Turn right at the top of the first field and then left over a stile. This path takes you past the wood and beyond this passes a water tower, some 200m to your right. This is the summit of Upton Beacon, the highest point of the day's walk. Continue along the track descending past a sports ground on the right. At the junction of tracks, go straight on down a narrow and steep back alley that leads between the houses. Go left at the wooden fence at the bottom to come out into Upton (21km)

Cross the small public garden on your right that leads to the road. Cross this and follow the well-defined path across reclaimed land. Where the path splits 200m further on, keep to the left, following it through the gate in the hedge ahead. The path passes under the stubby pylons and over the concrete bridge ahead. Veer right from here making for the church at the top of the hill. Cross two fields to come to the road leading past the church. Go right onto this road as far as T-junction 200m further on. Cross this and take the path almost immediately opposite, slightly to the left. Follow this path across four fields, going towards some warehouses, before emerging onto the next road.

Turn left here and follow the road to the crossroads (22.5km). Go straight over here into Mill Lane. On the right you can see the hills that form part of the next section of the West Yorkshire Way. Follow Mill Lane along and down to the next T-junction. Go right here steeply downhill to South Elmsall. The railway station is 0.5km further on, just before the main part of the town (23.5km). To continue the extra 1.5km to Moorthorpe Station, see the next chapter.

Southern Section – Walk One

South Elmsall to Darton

Route: South Elmsall – Hemsworth – Brierley – Shafton – Royston – Mapplewell – Darton

Distance: 23km; 14.5 ml

Ascent: 200m; 600 feet

Time: 5 – 7 hours

Maps: 1.25000 Pathfinders: 704 Hemsworth and Askern; 703 Wakefield (South) and Area; 715 Barnsley and Penistone. 1:50000 Landranger: 111 Sheffield and Doncaster

Getting There

South Elmsall and the neighbouring station of Moorthorpe are I.5km apart. Both stations lie along the route of the West Yorkshire Way, with Moorthorpe the more westerly of the two. They are on separate yet parallel train lines that join just to the north, and are served by trains from Leeds and Wakefield (Kirkgate). So there is a choice of going to either station, according to the convenience of the timetables. Trains run hourly to each station from Leeds and Wakefield on Mondays to Saturdays and every other hour on Sundays. For details of connections to and from Darton see the next walk.

The Day Ahead

This route passes across land that was once dominated by the coal industry. It skirts several old collieries and makes extensive use of the now dismantled railway network that used to serve the coal and mineral industries in this area. Although this cannot be described as the prettiest section of the route there is much attractive open countryside and farmland. Much of the interest in this walk lies in the wealth of industrial archeology and the diversity of the villages and towns that are passed. These vary from traditional mining villages, to villages such as Brierly and Shafton that are expanding with new housing development. In many of these villages there is much evidence of traditional Yorkshire leisure pursuits such as pigeon coops, racing dogs, fishing and lovingly-tended allotments.

The shops and pubs around here mostly cater for local people, as there are few tourists or day trippers. It makes a welcome change to be somewhere that isn't geared up to the tourist trade and where people often find the time of day to talk to visitors. There are cafes and pubs in Hemsworth and pubs in Brierley and Darton. To break the walk into more than a one day excursion, there are many bus links (too many to specify here) from Hemsworth, Brierley, Shafton and Royston running to Wakefield, Barnsley, Castleford, Knottingley and Doncaster.

From South Elmsall BR

Leaving South Elmsall station, turn left onto the road and cross the railway tracks. Turn right at the junction ahead and follow the High Street through the centre of South Elmsall. At weekends this is a bustling small shopping centre with a lively market, but in the evenings can be quite deserted. Keep on this road for approximately 2km. Half way along you pass a cemetery and over a railway line with Moorthorpe BR clearly visible from the road. Continuing along this road, you pass a small shopping parade and, 400m further on, reach a church with a tower on the left-hand side of the road. Turn right opposite the church into Northfield Lane (2km).

Go up this road and after 100m it swings to the left into a small housing estate. Keep along this road until it again swings to the left 300m further on. Continue straight ahead along the pedestrianised section for 20m to the signposted footpath along Hague Lane on the right. This path runs north east for more than 1km. At first it runs along a narrow lane between allotments, until coming out to an open field via a stile and footbridge (3km). Cross these and take the path going across the field towards the bank ahead. Once over the stile at the top, the path

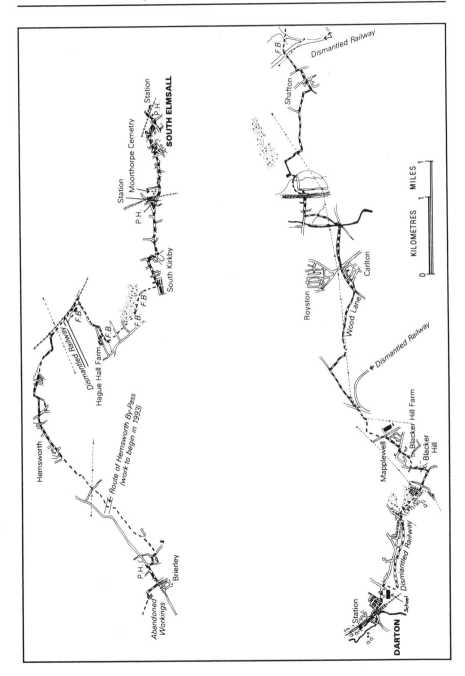

continues to rise over the crest of the small hill. From here the line of the path towards Hague Hill Farm becomes visible, dropping into a small valley (with a footbridge not yet visible) and rising over the brow of the hillock ahead. Once over the brow the path continues, crossing one track and coming out onto a road. The path continues on the opposite side of the road, through a gap in the hedge 10m to the right. Follow this down to the footbridge over the stream below (4km).

Once over the stream, follow the path to the right, along the field boundary around to the stile at the top right corner of the field. This leads into a small finger of woodland. Once through this veer right to follow the course of the stream. There is a steep bank on the far side of the stream marking the boundary of the now defunct colliery. Follow this path by the stream until it crosses the stream by a small footbridge and leads out to a broader track. The bank ahead is the embankment of the railway line. Turn left onto the track, and after 50m, climb the bank ahead, to come out next to the railway line (5km).

Continue following the railway line along for about 400m until a broad path comes in from the left (this is the route of a dismantled railway line). From here the path drops steeply from the embankment, still running parallel with the railway tracks. The path then starts to rise slightly and emerges on a broad gravel track between a sewerage farm and the railway track. From here the town of Hemsworth comes into view. After a short while the track turns away from the railway line and meets a tarmac track. Turn right onto this and follow it for almost 500m, crossing a bridge (6km) and then swinging towards Hemsworth on the left.

On reaching a corrugated metal fence at the edge of Hemsworth the track again turns sharply left. Turn off of it here and go straight over a patch of rough ground that leads to a metal stile 100m further on. Turn right after the stile and go immediately left onto a footpath between the houses. Follow this path as it crosses one quiet road and leads into a second residential street ahead. Follow this along turning sharply to the left after 200m. 100m further on, take the footpath to the right that runs between a metal fence and some fields to emerge on the main road through Hemsworth (7km)

Cross the road, and pick up the road slightly to the right on the opposite side. This has a small memorial garden on its right-hand side. Follow this road, rising steeply at first, and crossing a minor crossroads. Continue to go up past houses and then past playing fields. After 500m the road swings around to the right; carry straight on along a broad gravel track that takes you across open farmland. Follow this track for a further 500m until this also swings to the right towards a farmhouse. Again carry straight on, along a narrow, but well defined footpath passing under a row of pylons. From here the spire of Brierley Parish Church is clearly visible and provides a useful navigational aid. Continue along this footpath until it drops below the remnants of some rail embankments on the left. (This is soon to be the route of the Hemsworth by pass) (8.5km).

Shortly after the embankments, there is a junction of paths. Take the central path, running parallel with the road 100m to the right. Follow this path for about 400m until it meets a faint track, bordered by one line of trees. Cross the narrow field ahead, heading for the gap in the hedge at 11 o'clock. This leads to a broad track, turn right here and go past some farm buildings, to the road at Brierley. Turn right and follow the road round two bends before arriving at a T-junction. A strategically-located pub, The Three Horseshoes, on the corner of this junction marks a convenient lunch point (10km).

Cross the road at the junction and turn right along the main road (signposted towards Barnsley). Ignore the first footpath off to the right, but take the second footpath to the right 300m further on. Follow this downhill, towards the village of Shafton, which has just come into view. This track twists left and right and passes what appears to be an abandoned brickworks on the left. The path crosses a track (11km) (which is a branch of the same railway line that has been crossed already today), and continues to a stile and a gate leading to a field. Cross the field heading for the gate in the left-hand corner and the footbridge beyond (this crosses yet another disused railway line) and thence to the edge of Shafton. Turn left onto the road, then right at the first crossroads. Cross straight over the busy road at the T-junction and take the track opposite, rising slightly. After 100m this comes out at a junction of tracks (12km).

Old railway line near Shafton

Take the right-hand path and follow the fence along keeping the houses to your right. After 300m the track swings left onto the ridge of Gander Hill. After almost 1km, the town of Royston becomes visible ahead and the path starts to drop, passing under some pylons (13km). It then swings to the right towards the prominent, and barely-landscaped, slag heap ahead. As the path descends into the valley, it crosses a small footbridge and follows the line of a fence to the left. At the bottom of the valley, just before the unreconstructed lunar landscape, turn left following the same fence. This path soon leads out onto a broader track where you turn left and, keeping left at the only fork on this track, follow it to the railway lines. Some steps lead to a tunnel that will carry you safely under the tracks and to the edge of Royston (14km).

From the tunnel a small road leads straight ahead past a playground and houses. Take the second signposted bridleway to the left. This drops to a bridge over a small brook and then becomes a narrow footpath rising gently up Cronk Hill to the edge of the disused Barnsley Canal (15km). From here you can see the unusual tower of Carlton Parish Church. Cross the canal by the bridge and, follow the path, straight ahead. (This is another of those disused railway lines.) After 500m this leads to a road that you cross, continuing along the same path on the opposite side between fields and gardens. At the first junction of paths (16km) take the right-hand path rising to open fields. Pylons again serve as your markers and the path runs parallel with the high voltage line for almost 1km before swinging off to the right (17km).

300m after leaving the pylons behind, the path passes through a gate. Go left immediately after the gate towards a stile. Once over this, the path starts drawing closer to the pylons coming in from the left-hand side. Continue for just over 0.5km, crossing one path at right angles near the edge of the houses on your left. Carry straight on over this junction and along the edge of the field. Follow the path through a hedgerow to emerge on the bank of a disused railway line (18km). Turn left onto this track and, after 50m, take the faint path to the right leading from the embankment and towards the pylon on the right. Follow this to the pylon and beyond to the corner of the field, climbing a low stone bank into the next field. Follow the signpost towards the top corner of the hedgerow ahead and from here follow the faint, but signposted, footpath through some scrub land to the road ahead. Turn left and after 100m turn right through a gap in the hedge to bring you into a quiet suburban street (19km).

Keep to the right at the first minor junction and follow this street along for 200m to the T-junction. Cross the road and turn right. After 50m the road begins to dip and you take the footpath (signposted) to the left, running between the houses. A few steps along this path provides a wonderful view of Barnsley, with the hospital being the dominant concrete and glass building at the top of the hill. Follow this path for 100m to a metal gate. Turn right before the gate and drop 50m to a stile. Cross this and follow the right-hand path down the side of the hill to a second stone stile. From here go right and downhill to a third stile leading to the road. Turn left onto the road and follow it to Hill End Farm (20km). At the farmhouse the road veers right and heads for a T-junction 200m further on. Cross this road and take the signposted footpath across the colliery tip, heading towards the bottom corner of the houses ahead. Just before reaching the houses this path crosses a broader track (yet another disused railway line). Go straight across this, through the bicycle barrier and along the lane to the road ahead (21km).

Turn left onto the road then almost immediately after the road on the right (Rye Lane), go right, following the line of the disused railway track* which runs behind the houses. Follow this along for 1 km and take the third track leading off to the right (this is by the second break in the bank on the right hand side). Follow the path past some playing fields and a school on the left. Veer right by the school buildings, following the drive between the houses. At the road turn left and follow the road to a junction.

Keep to the left at this junction following this road along for a little over 1km to where it passes under a railway bridge. Immediately after the bridge turn right and follow this road for a short distance to the railway station at Darton (23km).

---

* This has recently been designated as a permissive right of way, thanks to the cooperation of British Coal Opencast and Barnsley MBC.

Southern Section – Walk Two

Darton to Denby Dale

Route: Darton – Haigh – Clayton West – High Hoyland – Swallow Hill –
Bagden Park – Denby Dale

Distance: 15km; 9.5ml

Time: 4 to 6 hours

Ascent: 420m; 1400ft

Maps: 1.25000 Pathfinders: 703 Wakefield (South) and Area; 715 Barnsley
and Penistone. 1:50000 Landranger: 110 Sheffield and Huddersfield

Getting There

Darton is on the Hallam Line which runs between Leeds and Sheffield
via Castleford, Wakefield (Kirkgate) and Barnsley. On Mondays to
Saturdays, trains run half hourly from Wakefield and hourly from Leeds
and Castleford. On Sundays they run hourly from all these stations. The
village of Darton lies within South Yorkshire, yet Darton is part of the
Metro network (presumably as it is the only station on this line between
Wakefield and Barnsley). So the fortunate residents of Darton have
access to the subsidised rail networks of both South and West Yorkshire.
From Huddersfield there is a direct bus service (235) to Darton, which
runs hourly. For details of return travel from Denby Dale see the next
section.

The Day Ahead

Although a short day, the hills of this area will make an impression,
especially after the comparative flatness of the last few sections.

However, it is not all hills and the first 3km provide a pleasant and easy stretch along the banks of the River Dearne. Once under the motorway at Hague, the path goes close to Bretton Hall and on to Clayton West from where the hills start to make themselves felt on the climb up to High Hoyland.

In the afternoon, the walk passes the seventeenth century farmhouse at Wheatley Hill and what is believed to be the only working pit left in West Yorkshire: the privately-run Hey Royd Colliery, tucked into the hillside. From here the path follows the ridge of the Dearne Valley, passing close to Blagden Hall before descending into Denby Dale. Denby Dale's claims to fame are its gigantic pies (the route passes one of the original pie dishes, now used as a flower bed) and the viaduct that is every bit as impressive as its more famous cousin in Ribblehead. Initially this was built from massive timber spars and resembled something from the Wild West. That structure was eventually declared unsafe and the present one was built alongside it in 1880.

This day's walk wanders between three boroughs, starting in Barnsley and criss-crossing several times into Wakefield and Kirklees. During the day the path follows stages of the Dearne Way, the Breeton Hall Trails and the Kirklees Way, also crossing the Cal-Derwent Way. The villages of Clayton West and High Hoyland provide convenient lunch points. These villages are also the most convenient points for breaking the walk into more than one excursion. The 235 bus passes through both villages linking Huddersfield and Barnsley. The 484 stops in Clayton West, linking Leeds and Wakefield in one direction, with Denby Dale and Holmfirth in the other. Both services run hourly.

From Darton BR

If coming from the Leeds/Wakefield direction, go right from the station to the road below and turn right through the tunnel under the railway line. Turn right at the junction beyond the tunnel and then left down a dirt track. 20 metres along this, turn right through a gap in the wooden fence, leading to open grassland. Much of this land used to be railway sidings for the collieries, but is now reinstated as a valuable piece of green belt. The path roughly follows the course of the River Dearne for about 3km, at first running across open grassland, and later farmland. The path is well walked as it forms part of the Dearne Way. After about

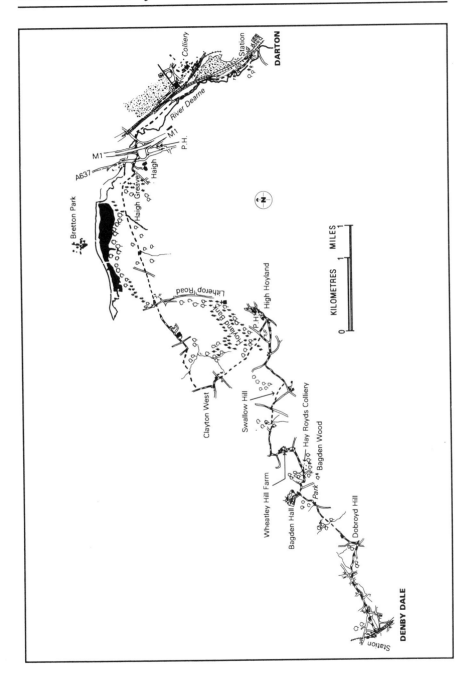

1km you pass the imposing, and now silent, structures of Wooley Colliery. From here the path crosses several fields before leading onto a broader drive and a road close to the junction of the M1 (3km).

Turn left onto the road, and follow it round to the right to take you across the roundabout under the M1 bridge. On the other side of the roundabout take the first road off to the right after the motorway slip road, leading to the Huddersfield Road. Take the first left into Jebb Lane leading to the hamlet of Haigh. At the time of writing, the Department of Transport has announced plans to build an M1 – M62 link motorway that will cut through this hamlet. The posters on street lamps and in peoples windows leave little doubt as to local opinion of this scheme. Follow the road through the village, following a sharp left bend. Just in front of the large barn on the right, take the footpath (signposted to Bretton Hall) off to the right, through a farmyard, gate and into grass pasture. The footpath follows the edge of the wood, turning to the left before rising slightly and leading to a stile. Cross the stile and follow the signposted path diagonally uphill across the field. This leads to a gap between two patches of woodland on the ridge of Oxley Bank (4.5km).

Once on top of the bank, the large transmitting tower at Emley Moor comes into view. This is going to remain in sight for much the rest of this walk and the next one, and will provide a useful navigational aid at times. Cross the double stile going left and following the waymarked Red Trail. This is signposted by wooden posts with red tops that provide useful markers for the next 1km. The path leads down the side of the bank, which provides good views of the Bretton Hall and glimpses of the lake below. Beyond the lake is the fascinating Yorkshire Sculpture Park. Continue to follow this path down the bank and then onto a broader track coming in from the right. Follow this along for 150 metres until it swings to the right where you follow the path to the left (marked by the red capped posts). Follow the path uphill to a stile, cross this and veer slightly left towards the fence ahead. Just before the fence cross a track (the route of the Cal Derwent Way), and go over the stile. Here you leave the red trail behind and follow the signposted footpath rising gently ahead. Quite suddenly you are on the brow of the hill with wonderful views over the hills beyond. Continue to the stile, and follow the footpath to the road below (6km).

Turn left at the road and 50 metres uphill go right onto the signposted footpath dropping across the field to a concrete footbridge. Continue uphill from here along the edge of the field to Clayton Hall Farm, visible at the top of the hill. Pass straight through the farmyard and follow the dirt track out. After 150m this track becomes tarmac and turns to the right, where it runs steeply downhill. The West Yorkshire Way carries straight on, through a stile on the left, signposted with a Kirklees Way symbol. Follow this path along the edge of the field to a stile in the corner (7km).

Care is needed here as three paths lead away from this stile. Take the middle path that runs directly towards the tower on Emley Moor. Follow this path over the brow of the hill and cross two stiles, then go left, following the hedge down towards some woods. Go through the woods and over the stream and take the left-hand path running next to the hedge. Follow this to the second stile where you turn left following the wooden fence along to a stile 200m further on. Cross this stile and follow the narrow footpath between the buildings and across a garden to come out onto a minor road. This is the very edge of Clayton West which lies to your right. Turn left onto the road and follow this to the right, passing a sign for Bilham Grange Farm. 100m further along, this track swings to the left. Take the footpath running straight ahead over a stile next to the five bar gate (8km).

Follow this path along the edge of the woods for 150m. At the end of a stone wall, carry straight on uphill. At the first stile the path begins to run parallel to the woods. Follow this over a further three stiles, after which it rises steeply through some woodland, and then crosses to the top left hand corner of the field ahead to come out to a green lane at the top of Hoyland Bank, the highest point of the day (9km).

From the top of this bank there are breathtaking views to the south. From here there is also a choice of routes. Right at this lane and right onto the road at the road below will lead along the shortest route. For a diversion to the very well-appointed pub at High Hoyland, go left and, after 50m, take the right-hand path over the bank. Follow the footpath down the edge of the field for 300m and drop down a ladder stile to the road. Turn left and The Cherry Tree is 100m along on the right. To regain the main route, turn back along the road and follow it along for 300m.

Follow the road along, past the first set of farm buildings on the right and at the next buildings take the road to the left that runs downhill. 300m down this road, go over a stile next to the second five-bar metal gate on the right-hand side. This is immediately under a line of wooden pylon posts. Follow the path to the crest of Swallow Hill (10km). The path veers slightly to the right of the line of pylons and again it's easy to use the transmitting tower at Emley as a guide to find the gap in the fence opposite. From the stile follow the path downhill as it runs back towards the pylons. Cross another stile and follow the path down towards the road. Turn left at the road and after 50m take the signposted footpath to the right. Follow this downhill to the corner of the wood ahead. Continue uphill following the path towards the metal gates (11km).

Once through these gates, go left, following the track towards Wheatley Hill Farm. Where the track turns to run parallel to the road, go through the gap in the wall on the right. Go left onto the road, passing the farm. In the midst of all the modern barns and outhouses, the farmhouse itself is a surprise: a half-timbered building dated 1651. Continue past the farmhouse, after which the road veers around sharply to the left. Immediately after this take the signposted footpath to the right past a gatekeeper's cottage (11.5km). This broad track leads towards, then around, Hays Edge Colliery a tiny working pit, tucked away in the edge of the woods. Follow the path past this and then through a muddy dip in the track and into the woods until coming to a junction of tracks by a cottage. Here you rejoin the Dearne Way and carry straight on for another 300m to the next cottage on the right. Go through the white kissing gate on the right after the cottage and follow the path down towards Lower Clough House. At the next kissing gate go straight on to the woods below and a third kissing gate (13km).

Drop through the woods, over a stile and follow the path straight over the field ahead. This leads to a stile, from where the path runs into a small field behind Stubbin House. Go through the field and pass the farmhouse, using the footpath between two walls to the left of the farm drive. The path rejoins the drive which you follow, around the flanks of Dobroyd Hill to the left. This then joins a wider track, passes a small wood on the right and does a sharp dogleg by a farmhouse before leading onto a road. Turn right onto the road and, after 100m, take a signposted footpath off to the right. Follow this down through the woods to the bottom of the hill. Cross the footbridge over the stream and turn left onto a gravel track. This leads out to Cuckstool Lane (14km). The name is a reminder of the barbarism of medieval times, when women suspected of witchcraft would have to undergo the horror of being submerged underwater in the ducking stool. Only the guilty were supposed to survive!

Turn right onto this road and follow it through to the main road. Turn left here towards the centre of Denby Dale. A little way along the main road you pass Pie Hall, built after the 1964 baking of the biggest pie in the world. The pie dish from then now acts as a flower bed in the front of the car park. It is almost 1km from here to the railway station. Drawing closer to the top of the town the viaduct looms ever larger and more impressive. Just before the viaduct the route to the station is signposted to the right (15km).

The viaduct at Dendy Dale

Southern Section – Walk Three

Denby Dale to Holme

Route: Denby Dale – Bird's Edge – Cheese Gate Nab – Jackson Bridge – Scholes Moor – Hollin Hill – Crow Hill – Ramsden Reservoir – Holme.

Distance: 19km; 12ml

Ascent: 525m; 1700ft

Time: $4^1/_2 - 6^1/_2$hr

Maps: 1:25000 Pathfinders: 715 Barnsley and Penistone; 714 Holmfirth and Saddleworth Moor. 1:50000 Landranger: 110 Sheffield and Huddersfield.

Getting There

Denby Dale is the last station in West Yorkshire on the Huddersfield – Sheffield line that runs through Penistone and Barnsley. Trains run hourly in each direction. This line is the most picturesque in West Yorkshire; the viaducts over the Colne and Holme Valleys giving wonderful views. If coming from Wakefield there is a direct bus service (484), which offers a speedier, if less spectacular approach to Denby Dale. For details of travel back from Holme see the next section.

The Day Ahead

We start to get into the higher country today. It is not only the landscape that starts to change but also the pattern of industry and settlements. This is one of the centres of Yorkshire's wool industry and the route passes a couple of mills located in steep wooded valleys. The villages that the route passes through have two distinct patterns, either clustered together in valley bottoms or spread out on the tops of the moors.

Starting at Denby Dale, in the shadow of its magnificent viaduct, the route starts by rising through woodland onto high open farmland. The path zigzags along minor roads for 3km before dropping gently from the moors towards Jackson Bridge. This provides the most convenient stopover point for lunch, and also for access back to Huddersfield or Holmfirth for those who prefer a shorter walk.

From Jackson Bridge, the route passes around the back of Hepworth Church, before entering the tranquil nature reserve at Morton Woods. Climbing from the top of this valley to the southern end of Scholes Moor the route drops to Hollin Reservoir and its surrounding forestry. From here there is another stretch of open land before dropping into the forests around Ramsden Reservoir. Although a completely man-made landscape, its grace and beauty provide one of the highlights of the West Yorkshire Way.

From Denby Dale BR

From the platform go down the steps and under the subway. Follow the path to the gravel road below. Turn left and then immediately right down a flight of steps to the road below. From here there is an unsurpassed view along the length of the viaduct crossing the Dearne Valley. Cross the road and follow the flight of steps down, parallel with the viaduct, passing Hinchcliffe Mills. Turn right half way up the bank and follow the chain link fencing around the edge of the mills. Once past the mill the path turns left and rises past a terrace of houses to lead out to the road. Turn right onto the road and after 250m left onto a woodland track (1km).

Follow this track uphill through these mature beech wood. Where the track turns to the left towards Wood Farm, go through the kissing gate ahead and follow the footpath across the top of the meadow. Keep to the top path and follow this to the stile at the end of the field. From here head for the gap in the wall straight ahead, by the top of the wood, and follow the path straight on keeping close to the wall. After 200m this brings you out onto a track that leads to New House Farm (2.5km). Continue along the same track to bring you to Bird's Edge Farm and

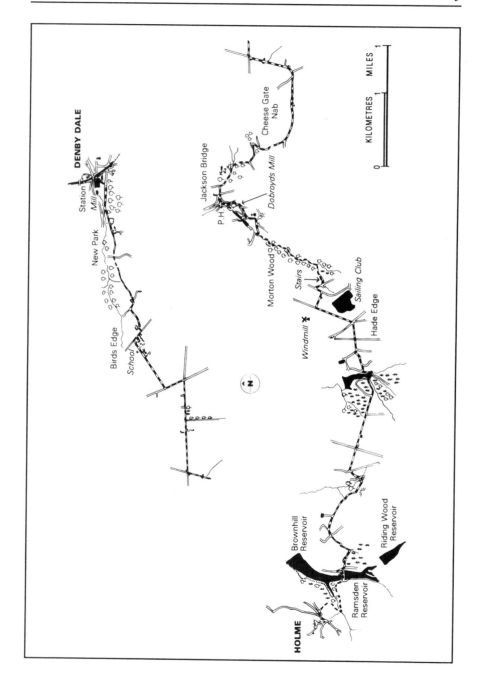

onto the road in Bird's Edge (3km).

Go right here and then take the first road on the left, Bird's Edge Lane, which leads past a school, a Wesleyan chapel and on into open country. Continue along this lane to the first T-junction and turn left (4km). Follow this road for 300m to a crossroads and turn right onto Windmill Lane. The name of this road probably precedes the modern wind turbine that (on a clear day) you can see ahead on Scholes Moor. This road also forms part of the boundary between South and West Yorkshire. Go gently uphill for just over 1km, past one set of farmhouses to a second group of houses by a crossroads. Go left here and follow the road down to the second set of farm buildings ahead at Hey Slack (6km).

Just after this farm house the road curves around to the right, then turns sharply left. Go right at the bend onto a minor road and, after 50m, take the drive off to the left, signposted for Upper Millshaw Hall. After the last hour or so of road walking it makes a pleasant change to get back onto rough tracks again. Follow the track along and, just before the farmhouse, take the higher path to the right. Continue to contour around the edge of Cheese Gate Nab, the hill to your right. After 500m this broad track drops away steeply towards Hepworth. Turn right at this point onto a smaller path which climbs over a bank before descending gently around the side of the hill. This beautiful pathway runs for about 500m to a stone stile leading to a rough track (7.5km).

Turn left here and follow the track, as it zig zags around the edge of the woods before descending sharply downhill. At the bottom, go right and follow the drive along, past some woods and over a small stream to lead out to the edge of Jackson Bridge. Go left at the T-junction with the minor road, over the cross roads ahead, and straight down the hill to the centre of the village (9km). Some may recognise the inn ahead (The White Hart) as Compo and the gang's local in "Last of the Summer Wine".

Go left at the crossroads following the road along the edge of the walled river towards the mill complex on your right-hand side. Just above the mills take the footpath off to the right, signposted for the Mill Shop. This climbs steeply up a bank, leading to the edge of Dobroyd Mills. Pass the shop and the mills on your right-hand side and go straight on towards the yellow and black road barrier ahead, (ignoring the drive off to the

Morton Woods, near Hepworth

left). Follow this drive for 100m until it turns sharply to the right. Go straight on here, onto the footpath through the woods. This leads past some attractive new housing on the right and past the entrance to Hepworth Parish Church on the left (10km).

Turn right at the road ahead and follow it down to the next valley. After 200m, the road turns sharply to the right. Just after this bend, take the footpath to the left leading into the woods. You are now back on the Kirklees Way and on one of the most delightful stretches of these walks. This path twists and turns, rises and falls, and crosses the river several times along 1.5km of wonderfully unspoilt valley bottom. The valley contains many different species of trees, a profusion of ferns and mosses and is rich with bird and insect life. A couple of spectacular cliffs drop away to the valley floor. It is difficult not to linger in this pleasant shady spot. Approaching the head of the valley, the path climbs a bank to a wooden staircase that leads out to a drive by a small group of cottages (12km).

Turn right onto the drive and follow it up to the road. Go left at the top, and 100m on turn right onto the signposted footpath. This path leads across a field to a small farm house on the top of Scholes Moor. To the left of this path you can see a reservoir, used by a sailing club. The path passes to the right of the farmhouse and, once past the side of the house, you can see sails of a different kind. The windmill that you saw earlier in the day looms 200m ahead on the horizon. This is the power source for Longley Farm, and the first of its kind in the county. Opinions vary as to whether it adds or detracts from the environment. Personally I find its grace inspiring and perhaps a sign of things to come as we belatedly realise the damage that fossil fuels are causing to the atmosphere.

Follow the path up towards the wind turbine and onto Scholes Moor Road. Turn left and follow the road gently downhill, past the sailing club towards the crossroads (13km). Cross the road with care and carry straight on into Greave Road. Though almost a thousand feet up, this part of the moor around Hade Edge is surprisingly well populated. Carry straight on, through the village, over the first crossroads and past the school. When the road begins to drop away to the right, cross the ladder stile on the left (signposted for the Kirklees Way). Follow the path downhill, keeping the dry stone wall to your right. Near the bottom of the hill cross a stile and follow the path to the drive below. Go left here following this track to the head of the reservoir (14km).

Follow the track in a clockwise direction around the reservoir, crossing three small bridges. When the track starts to rise, turn sharply left, onto what looks like a minor footpath (signposted for the Kirklees Way). This narrow path climbs for about 300m through heather and bracken towards the top of Reynard Clough, before turning right into the edge of a plantation. Some 50m further on, this path leads to a broad green track. Turn left here and go straight on for 1.5km. This leads through the plantation, out into open grazing land, past farm buildings, across a broad dirt track (where the Kirklees Way turns off to the left) (15.5km) and continues on to a minor road.

Go left here and, almost immediately, take the path signposted off to the right. This drops towards the head of a small clough. Cross the stream at the head of the clough (16km) and follow the path round the top of the woods. From here there are views across to the hills above Holmfirth and the executive housing climbing up the sides of those same hills. Castle Hill is also clearly visible further to the right. Continue following this path as it contours around the hill, crossing one stream bed and a private lane leading off to Moss Edge Farm on the right (17km).

Shortly after the farm the path runs between two dry stone walls and enters the northern edge of the Peak District National Park. At the end of this narrow lane the paths diverge. Take the lower footpath and keep straight on keeping close to the dry stone wall to your right, ignoring the path that drops away sharply to the right after 100m. Continue to the edge of the forest at Tinker Well. Go over the ladder stile and follow the edge of the forest down towards the reservoir. Go right at the road and after 100m turn sharp left onto the path that runs between the two reservoirs. At the end of the causeway follow the railings to the right to lead into the woodland (18km).

This last section of today's walk through the forest provides one of the highlights of the entire West Yorkshire Way. Passing over the crest of the hill, look between the trees to see the calm waters of the reservoir below. This path runs through the forest for 0.5km, doubling back on itself to cross a feeder stream via a footbridge. Shortly after the footbridge the path emerges into open meadowland. Keep to the bottom of the first field and then go diagonally uphill across the second one. The path goes left here, along the edge of two more fields to come out on the road in Holme.

Just before reaching the road you may notice an elevated lawn with plastic bubbles set in it. Don't rub your eyes too hard: the domes are skylights, and the lawn is the over-roof insulation of a house built into the edge of a bank, appropriately named Underbank. At the road go left to bring you to the centre of the village (19km).

Buses back to Holmfirth and Huddersfield run from the cobbled triangle 100m up the road. A few metres beyond here is The Fleece – a popular walker's pub.

Western Section – Walk One

Holme to Marsden

Route: Holme – Marsden Clough – Wessenden Head – Marsden Moor – Marsden

Distance: 13km; 8ml

Ascent: 280m; 950ft

Time: 3 – 4^1/$_2$ hours

Maps: 1.25000 Pathfinders: 714 Holmfirth and Saddleworth Moor; 702 Huddersfield and Marsden. 1:50000 Landranger: 110 Sheffield and Huddersfield

Getting There

Holme is at the top of the Holme valley on the road to Holme Moss, just 3 miles past Holmfirth. There is no train station at this remote village, perched on the edge of the moors. But, there is a regular bus service (310/312) which runs hourly from Huddersfield every day of the week including Sundays. For details of public transport links from Marsden see the next chapter.

The Day Ahead

This is a short but pleasant day's walk across moorland and along high valleys that have been dammed to create a series of spectacular reservoirs. Nearly all of the walk is within the boundaries of the Peak District National Park, and follows easily recognisable tracks for nearly all of its route. Because of the elevated position of Holme (at almost 1000ft) the early ascent to the tops is far less strenuous than might be expected. Indeed, the first mile is slightly downhill towards the first of the many reservoirs that we pass today.

Wessenden Head, at 415m, is the highest point of the day, and this is reached within three miles of leaving Holme. Here, the West Yorkshire Way joins up with the Pennine Way. It follows a broad, well-surfaced track around the side of four reservoirs that lead to the edge of Marsden.

There is very little in the way of civilisation along this route. There are neither refreshment stops nor public transport links between the start and end of this walk. The only road that is crossed is the high level route over the moors at Wessenden Head. It is essential to go properly equipped for high level walking as the weather can be very changeable on these tops, even if the weather appears clement on starting out.

From Holme Village

Cross the cobbled triangle opposite the bus stop, passing a small play area on your left. Shortly after this there is a minor road junction. Immediately after this take the footpath through the gate on the right-hand side. This path leads between two walls and then into open fields. It is part of the Kirklees Way and is well signposted and clearly defined. Follow this waymarked footpath across five fields. After the second field Digley Reservoir and the shadow of Marsden Clough, (which you will later follow), come into view and the path starts dropping gently. After the fifth field, the path drops more steeply towards the reservoir, crosses a footbridge and one more field before dropping to a steep bank that leads to the causeway across the dam over Bilberry Reservoir (1.5km).

The view from here across Bilberry Reservoir, with its steep rocky sides, inlets running off to the distance, and the heather moors above is one of the finest on the entire West Yorkshire Way. Follow the path across the dam over the reservoir, then climb up to the left to a metal gate. At the gate turn right onto the track ahead and climb steeply for 100m before turning left onto a broad track, just above a wooden bench. This track climbs gently for about three hundred metres before turning sharply right and climbing more steeply to a junction of tracks. Turn left here and follow this track for about 1.5km, again climbing gently towards the head of Marsden Clough, passing two sets of farm buildings on the way.

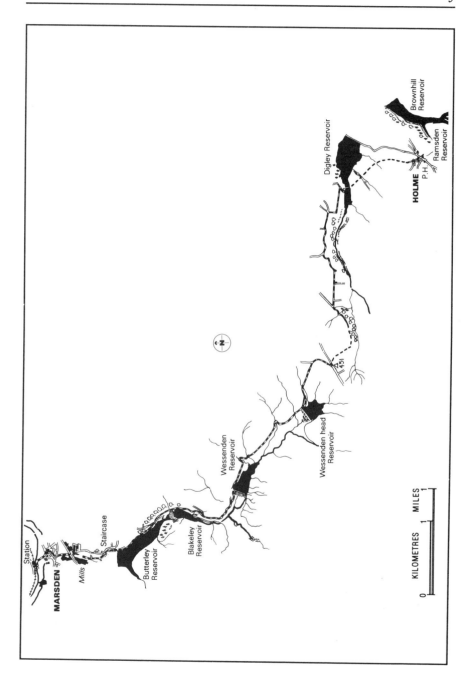

Bilberry Reservoir, near Holme

Eventually the track comes out at a T-junction, where the main track veers off to the right to the road above (4km).

Go left here, crossing the ladder stile (waymarked for the Kirklees Way). Follow this track past the top of some woods which, after 300m, begin to drop away to the left. Keep to the same footpath as it continues straight on and then rises to the right, towards Wessenden Head, and the road running over the tops. Cross the ladder stile to the road and turn left. Almost immediately you will see a road coming in from the right. Turn onto this and follow it along for 300m to a track running off to the left (signposted 'Pennine Way') (5.5km).

From here the path couldn't be simpler – just follow the track down along this broad elevated valley for almost 6km. Following the twists and turns in the track the path leads past four reservoirs on the way to Marsden. With so little navigating to do there is ample time to look around and enjoy the rapidly changing scenery. Footbridges take you over a couple of fast running streams. The steep cuts in the hills opposite reveal more streams and rivulets, complete with waterfalls, flowing into the valley bottom. Continuing to descend, the path runs past reservoir heads with original Victorian Gothic architecture.

500m after the second reservoir, Wessenden Reservoir, The Pennine Way is signposted, dropping off to the left towards the valley bottom (9km). Ignore this and continue down the main track, passing two more reservoirs on your descent. Above the last of these reservoirs Butterley Reservoir, the track comes out onto a road where it leaves The National Park. Just a few metres along this road, take the footpath off to the left, passing through a gate. This leads onto a steep stairway cut into the hillside. At this point you can be thankful that you are going down!

At the bottom of the stairs, turn right onto the footpath that leads past some cottages on your left, cutting through a mill complex on either side of the path. Once past the mills, turn left onto the road and go straight over the cross roads ahead, toFalls Road. After 200m this road splits, and you take the lower left-hand fork that carries you safely under the busy Manchester Road. Once through the tunnel the road runs parallel with the river, and soon leads to the town centre. From the square you can see the interesting Germanic design of the tower on the Mechanics Institute to your right.

The station is a little way away from the town centre. To find it, follow the river along to the bridge, cross this and turn left. The road rises, turning to the right, with the station 200 metres uphill on the far side of the canal (13km).

Western Section – Walk Two

Marsden to Todmorden

Route: Marsden – Willykay Clough – White Hill – Blackstone Edge – Light Hazzles Edge – Warland Reservoir – Walsden

Distance: 24km; 15ml

Ascent: 450m; 1500ft

Time: 6 to 8 hours

Maps: This is one of those walks where you start on the corner of one map, cut across a corner of a second and end up on a third. Normally 1:50000 maps are adequate for these walks. On this route, however, the larger scale maps are essential. The Outdoor Leisure Map for the South Pennines (21) covers most of today's walk as well as the next two walks, so is a good investment.

The relevant maps (in both sizes) are:

1:50000 Sheffield and Huddersfield (110), Greater Manchester (109), Blackburn and Burnley (103). 1:25000 Huddersfield and Marsden (702), Bury, Rochdale and Littleborough (701), South Pennines (Outdoor Leisure 21).

Getting There

Marsden is a 15 minutes train journey from Huddersfield. Trains run hourly from Wakefield via Huddersfield. Buses link Marsden to Huddersfield and the lower Colne Valley, also to Oldham.

The Day Ahead

This is a magnificent high level walk linking the last towns in the Colne and Calder Valleys. Much of the day is spent above 1000 ft, and a good deal of the time is spent following the Pennine Way. Although this has the reputation as the "motorway" of long distance footpaths it can still be easy to lose your way, especially if the weather changes abruptly. It is essential to go well prepared: a map and compass and the ability to use them are important. These moors offer few landmarks and in poor visibility a compass is essential for safe navigation.

It is also important to be prepared for all weathers: Waterproof and warm clothing are essential and, in the summer, sun cream might be a good idea as there is little shelter; the effects of the sun are all too easily masked by the wind and only felt later. It can be very muddy and slippery on these moors, so unless the weather has been very dry, or is frosty, gaiters will be an advantage. Despite all these warnings, this is one of the most exhilarating parts of the walk. Thousands have trod this path as part of their Pennine Way pilgrimage, yet for all that there remains a real feeling of wilderness when you get onto the tops.

Despite the remoteness of the countryside through which this route passes, there are several points at which the journey can be broken if so wished. The following points all offer access to public transport links:

A672 (near motorway junction). Hourly bus service (562) between Oldham and Halifax.

A58 (near White House public house). Hourly bus service (527/528/561) between Rochdale and Halifax.

Walsden. Train service between Manchester (via Rochdale) and Leeds (via Todmorden, Halifax and Bradford). See details in next chapter.

There are also a couple of refreshment stops available along the route. The layby on Windy Hill, near the M62 (9km) has a caravan selling teas and snacks whose owner claims to be there every day of the year. His clientele is a mix of HGV drivers and Pennine Way walkers. The White House on the A58 (15km) is a CAMRA recommended pub. Their food is good, but no meals are served after 2.30 and no drinks after 3.00.

Walsden has a fish shop and a couple of pubs. In Todmorden, however, you are spoilt for a choice of good pubs and reasonable eating places.

From Marsden BR

From Marsden station turn right onto the road and follow this over the railway bridge away from town. Immediately over the bridge, turn left following the sign for the New Hey Hotel. Follow this quiet road all the way along to the hotel (2km). Just after the hotel where the road rises steeply, take the signposted footpath to the left, through a gate and onto a muddy track along the river bank. Follow this for 300m to Close Gate Bridge at the edge of Marsden Moor. Take the hint and remember to close the gate behind you.

Close Gate bridge

Take the right-hand path along the bottom of the clough and after 100m or so follow the track steeply uphill towards Willykay Clough. After a short steep climb, this comes out onto a plateau of moorland with few

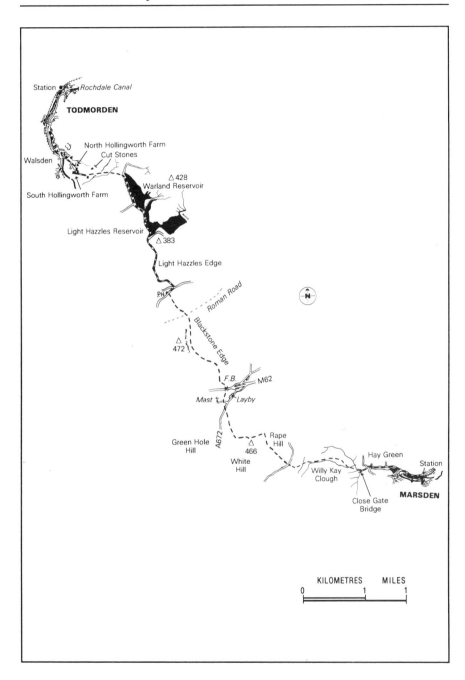

distinguishing features. Follow this well used footpath WNW for 750m
then WSW for a similar distance. A short steep climb just after a small
waterfall leads to a junction of tracks. The broader of these is the
Pennine Way. Follow this well-defined path down to the road below.,
the A640, which you cross (5.5km)

The path is well signposted on the other side of the road and climbs
slowly to the top of Rape Hill. The path is well worn, occasionally giving
way to quagmire. From the broad summit the path drops a little, fording
a couple of small streams and climbs gently again towards Linsgrave
Head. On a clear day the radio mast gives a good bearing for this
section. From the head, follow the signs pointing to the right bringing
you to the trig point at the summit of White Hill. From here continue
gently downhill in a westerly direction for 600 yards until the path turns
northwards towards the tower ahead. Just before the tower the path
crosses the A672 Oldham/Halifax road.

There is a layby here usually with a mobile cafe parked up.
Unfortunately the layby is also a favourite fly-tipping spot so is not the
prettiest of places, even if the refreshment break is welcome. From here,
the Pennine Way footpath is clearly signposted, going out of the back of
the layby. This path leads to the footbridge high above the M62. After
the silence of the moors it is disquieting to be walking sixty feet or so
above the roar of traffic on the main trans-Pennine road link. This brief
encounter with civilisation marks the approximate half way point of the
day's excursion (10km).

From the end of the motorway bridge the path is clearly visible as it
rises to the NW. After a short steep climb, there is a slow and hardly
perceptible rise towards the top of Blackstone Edge, 2km from the
motorway. In sunshine or mist Blackstone Edge is spectacular, an
exposed ledge of wind-eroded millstone grit. The trig point, marking the
highest end of the ridge is at the southern end, and from there you
follow the ridge northwards. Coming off the ridge, pass through a
narrowly-spaced pair of pillars that leads onto the 'Roman Road' that
runs NE-SW (12.5km).

Crossing over this ancient highway, take the path running NW that
drops quite steeply over the edge of Blackstone Edge Moor and onto a
well-defined water company track. Following this round to the right

brings you on to the Oldham/Halifax road. A right turn here soon brings you up to the CAMRA recommended "White House" 100m uphill (14km).

One hundred yards uphill from the Inn the Pennine Way turns left away from the road and onto another well defined water company track. It is flat walking for a good way now, skirting around the edge of several reservoirs. The broad track and the lack of gradient make for easy going, on what is the last high level stretch of today's walk. After 1.5km the tracks diverge; ignore the one to the right (signposted Reservoir Circuit). Keep to the left and you soon reach the northern edge of Warland Reservoir, the third and final reservoir along this stretch. Cross the fine stone bridge and leave the Pennine Way behind by taking the path to the left (18km).

Follow this due west, dropping gradually at first and then more steeply. After 1km, follow the posts to the right that provide a guide to the footpath that leads back to the valley below. Eventually this path drops down to Hollingworth Gate. Turn right here and pass South Hollingworth Farm. From the farmhouse, take the drive that contours around the hill towards North Hollingworth Farm. Here the track starts to drop steeply down towards Walsden. Just after the first stone cottages on the right, a cobbled ginnel drops steeply to the left; this brings you to the valley bottom, just in front of the churchyard (20.5km)

From here it is an easy walk, following the canal path for the last 3km into Todmorden. This stretch provides an interesting contrast to the day spent on the tops. The river, canal, road and railway line cross over and under each other along the length of this narrow valley bottom. There is a fine Gothic Victorian bridge at Gauxholme, and beyond this, a breathtaking embankment dropping at least 100 ft from the railway line to the canal below. On arriving at Todmorden, turn left onto the main road, then left again for the railway station.

Rochdale Canal, Todmorden

Western Section – Walk Three

Todmorden – Haworth

Route: Todmorden – Blackshawhead – Walshaw Lodge – Top of Stairs – Oxenhope – Haworth

Distance: 25km; 15.5ml

Ascent: 700m; 2300ft

Time: 6 – 9 hours

Map: 1:25000 Outdoor Leisure 21 – South Pennines. 1:50000 Landranger: 103 Blackburn, Burnley and surrounding area; 104 Leeds and Harrogate

Use of the Outdoor Leisure map is strongly recommended for this walk.

Getting There

Todmorden is the last stop but one in West Yorkshire along the Calder Valley line. Direct trains run from Leeds via Bradford and Halifax on a half-hourly basis every day of the week. Buses run from Burnley and Rochdale (half-hourly), Halifax and Hebden Bridge (half hourly). There is also an occasional bus service (500) from Keighley to Todmorden via Haworth and Hebden Bridge. This runs four times a day: daily through the summer but on only Wednesdays and Saturdays throughout the rest of the year. For details of transport from Haworth see the next walk.

The Day Ahead

This section is mostly on high moorland but also traverses several steep wooded valleys. Once again it is essential to go prepared for bad weather as it can be very changeable on these tops. The walk offers wonderful views and dramatic changes of scenery from moortop to steep cloughs and fast flowing streams.

Starting in Todmorden the route quickly gains height and after a short while links up with the Calderdale Way. It follows this path past Great Rock, through Blackshawhead and onto to Colden Clough. From here, the West Yorkshire Way follows the route of the Pennine Way as far as Green Hill. It then turns onto local paths towards the High Greenwood entrance to Hardcastle Crags. Traversing the steep sides of this local beauty spot, the path rises to Walshaw Lodge and out onto open moors. From here, clear straight paths lead around Shackleton Knoll, down to Grain Water Bridge and back up to Top of Stairs, the highest point of the day. From here the route descends over moorland and around hilltop farms to Oxenhope and for the last stretch follows the banks of the River Worth to Haworth.

This is one of the longer sections of the walk. It is approximately the same length as the previous walk, but involves more ascent and, for the first half at least, more intricate map work. For those who wish to break the walk into more than one day's excursion there are several convenient points to do so. These nearly all involve using footpaths that lead back to Hebden Bridge. The most convenient routes run from the top of Colden Clough, from Hardcastle Crags, and from Hardibut Clough. Once past the last of these, you are effectively committed to two or three hours over exposed moorland, so leave sufficient time and reserves of energy for the last section.

Bus routes are passed at Blackshawhead where the H2 provides an hourly service to Hebden Bridge (two-hourly service on Sundays). There is also a bus service from Hardcastle Crags to Hebden Bridge (H8), though there are only four a day on Mondays to Saturdays with no Sunday service. Buses from Shaw and Oxenhope provide links to Haworth, Keighley and Bradford.

Todmorden offers opportunities for slap-up breakfasts, (a favourite of mine is the Market Cafe opposite the bus station). From there, refreshment stops are limited to pubs near the start and the end of the day. The route passes near two pubs a few miles from the start: the Shoulder of Mutton at Blackshawhead, and the New Delight at Jack Bridge. There are no further watering holes until Oxenhope, quite near the end of the day. Here there is a pub (The Bay Horse) and a couple of shops. Haworth has enough tearooms, fish and chip shops and inns to satisfy most people's tastes. As a popular tourist destination, Haworth can seem quite frantic after the desolation of the moors.

From Todmorden BR

From the railway station, descend to the main road and turn left towards the splendid railway viaduct. Go under the viaduct and take the first road on the right, Stansfield Road. Follow this along for 500m to a minor crossroads, just after which the older housing gives way to newer houses. Go right here up a short cul-de-sac to cross the footbridge over the railway line. Pass a playground on the right and turn right onto the road ahead. Follow the road past Stansfield Hall on your left (1km).

When the road veers to the right, go left up the unmade road, by the pillar box. Follow this around two bends until you get to the third group of cottages. A signpost points you along the edge of the drive of the first of these cottages and then along a path going steeply uphill for about 500m. Turn left at the top of the hill and follow the broad track along for about 400m, passing Todmorden Golf Course on the right. This track offers great views across Todmorden and along the valley leading towards to Cornholme. Shortly before the track drops to a junction, the route joins the Calderdale Way, passing through a hole in the wall on the right-hand side (2.5km).

Follow this path as it rises past some ramshackle farm outhouses. Once onto the brow of the hill the path becomes more clearly defined, crossing several fields and passing close to the boundary of the golf course on the right. Some 200m after the golf course, the path comes out onto a road. Turn left and then go right into a farm yard (3km). The path passes through the farmyard and out through a gap in the wall at the far end. From here the path contours along the side of the Calder Valley, crossing several fields and three enclosed paths. This eventually leads to a stream and immediately after this turns left, up a bank before leading to a broad track. Turn right onto this and follow it to the road. Go left and then right at the junction 100m further up bring you to Great Rock (5km).

From here the route turns away from the Calder Valley, following the well-signposted path to the left towards Hippins Bridge. This provides a

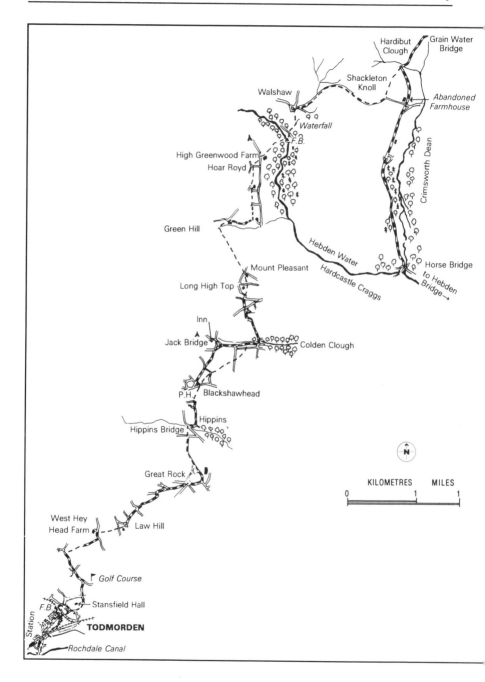

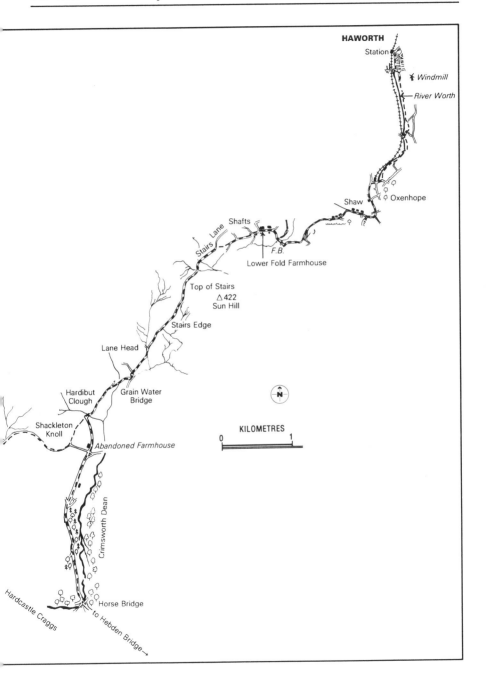

gentle descent towards the road which becomes steep just before meeting the road. Turn left at the road, go over the bridge and then right towards Hippins (6km). This is an outstanding 17th century cottage with well preserved mullioned windows. From the cottage take the signposted path to the left towards Lower Blackshawhead. The path passes three farmhouses and for a while is made up of large stone setts, laid across a stream, which can be heard flowing underfoot. After heavy rain the stream is more evident, running around the side and over the tops of the stones! The path emerges in Blackshawhead next to the former Post Office (6.5km).

Blackshawhead

From here there is the possibility of two small detours to the only hostelries that will be found until near the end of the day's route. 200m along, the road to the left leads to the Shoulder of Mutton. Alternatively cross the road opposite the former post office, and take the small road in front. Turn right downhill going straight ahead onto a grass track when the road veers left. Turning right onto the road and round the dogleg will bring you out to the famous New Delight at Jack Bridge. This little detour runs almost parallel to the main route, so adds little distance to the day.

To keep to the West Yorkshire Way, follow the signposted track through the hole in the wall opposite the former Post Office. This footpath, mostly laid with stone setts, descends gently downhill, cutting diagonally across six fields before crossing a track. Turn left here and follow the track to the farmhouse below. Turn right by the farm towards the next farmhouse along the track and then turn left onto the footpath leading downhill. This leads to another track where you go right, following it for 100m to the footpath on your left, dropping steeply down the side of Colden Clough to the footbridge below (8km).

Cross the old clapper bridge at the bottom. Half way up the bank rising from Colden Clough, the Calderdale Way splits off to the right. (It is possible to return to Hebden Bridge from here by following the Calderdale Way along the top edge of this valley to Heptonstall and thence to Hebden Bridge via Hell Hole Rocks). Here you carry straight on uphill following the acorn signs that denote the Pennine Way.

As the incline eases, the path leads to a farm where a faded PW sign on the wall ahead directs you to the left towards the farmhouse. Go over the stile and then right along the track leading to the Slack Road. Cross straight over this and onto a recently resurfaced footpath going uphill. Cross the next road, 100m ahead, and continue up the track to the first farmhouse, Long High Top. Pass this on your right and continue over the brow of the hill to a second farmhouse at Mount Pleasant (9km). From here the path is well-cairned and runs to the left across open moorland towards Green Hill. It then drops to the abandoned farmhouse visible at Clough Head (10km).

From here, the West Yorkshire Way leaves the Pennine Way for the last time and drops through a gap in the dry stone wall on the right, heading towards the abandoned farmhouse. Follow the footpath past the house, keeping it on your right. Go through a gate and follow the dry stone wall downhill for 50m. At the next wall there are two gates, pass through the lower one and follow the broader path down the side of the valley to the farmhouse below. Just before the farmhouse, take the top footpath to the left signposted for High Greenwood and Widdop Road.

This path runs above the first farmhouse and then contours around the side of the hill. It passes two more farmsteads, goes over Pisser Clough, and onto a third group of farm buildings at Hoar Royd (11km).

Cross the top of the farm track here and go through the five-bar gate beyond. Looking back from here there are wonderful views along the top of Hardcastle Crags. Take the footpath that runs diagonally across the field towards a camping and caravan site at High Greenwood Farm. Cross the road to the tarmac entrance to the farm, go along this drive for a few metres and go left through a five-bar gate next to a barn. The signpost here is well-camouflaged and indicates a path running diagonally across two fields and leading to the High Greenwood entrance to Hardcastle Crags (11.5km).

Hardcastle Crags is a magnificent fertile and steeply-sloped wooded valley stretching some three miles from the barren moorland at Black Dean. The West Yorkshire Way cuts straight across this ribbon of woodland. Those wishing to explore it more fully can take the gently sloping track to the right; following the valley bottom will bring you to Horse Bridge and then Hebden Bridge.

From the entrance to the woods, cross the track and drop straight down the steep slopes of the valley to the footbridge below. Cross the bridge and take the path to the left, crossing a small stone footbridge 200m further on. Immediately after this take the smaller path to the right that rises steeply uphill towards the top of the woods. This is quite a demanding climb but one that is accompanied by the sounds of a waterfall, which you can catch glimpses of from the top of the hill. Nearing the top of the woods the main path turns to the right. Go left following a smaller path through bracken to a gate 100m on. Go through this and follow the path uphill across an open field leading to Walshaw Lodge (12.5km).

Follow the signs into and over the farmyard to the junction of tracks beyond. Turn right here and, after 30m, take the bridleway, signposted to Crimsworth Dean that runs off to the left. After 300m the path begins to follow the line of a dry stone wall that skirts the edge of Shackleton Knoll. Keep to this wall, following it round around the edge of the hill. After half a kilometre, the path passes through the wall and continues to skirt around the hill. Ignore the first footpath off to the right 0.5km further on. Follow the wall for a further 250m until the path passes through it and drops down to Hardibut Clough on the track below (15km).

Hardibut Clough is hardly a great landmark, but offers a choice of routes. Turning left you continue along the West Yorkshire Way onto the open moors and a further $2^1/_2$ – $3^1/_2$ hours walk to Haworth. Turning right will lead to the mouth of Hardcastle Crags and back to Hebden Bridge in a little more than an hour (see map for details). Your decision will depend on the weather and your level of fitness.

To continue towards Haworth turn left and follow this broad footpath running gently and then more steeply downhill to Grain Water Bridge (16km). From the bridge follow the track up to the road junction and then go left, following the double dog-leg and then rising extremely steeply to pass the lane that leads to Whitehole Farm on the right. The road rises less steeply from here to Lane Head, where the tarmac road turns towards the farm buildings on your right. Carry straight on uphill along the rough track. A further 1km of gentle climbing leads to "Top of Stairs", the highest and bleakest point of the day (17km). If the weather is fine it feels like you are climbing into the sky. From the top, there are views of Worth Valley, Ilkley Moor, and the Southern Dales. If the weather is less than fine you may literally find your head in the clouds.

Follow the broad track down from the top. After 300m the path passes a clough with a spectacular landslip and then passes through a gate. Continue to descend for a further 300m to where the track broadens and veers to the left. From here, very careful navigation is required. Go through the hole in the wall on the right and straight across the field ahead. These fields are full of broken down dry stone walls. At the first junction of walls, go straight on, heading for the prominent windmill ahead. Follow the line of walls downhill for 300m to an abandoned building (marked as shafts on map). Keep this on the left and continue descending to the farmhouse below (18.5km).

Cross the stone stile at the very corner of the field next to the farmhouse and go right along the track, past the farmhouse to a junction. Cross straight over this, passing a second group of farmhouses on your left. You are now approaching a sign for Lower Fold that tells you to keep out and warns of dangerous dogs. Don't panic! Between the bottom of the cottages to your left and the entrance to the farm there is a green lane. Turn onto this enclosed pathway and follow it for more than 2km. It eventually leads to the edge of Shaw. This lane skirts around one side of the clough, crosses the stream and contours around the other side of the clough before rising to the edge of the bracken bank on the right. The lane follows the bottom of this bank around until it drops you in Shaw Lane (21.5km).

Go right here and then left at the main road. Follow this round as it swings to the left, past the Bay Horse. When the road swings to the right, go straight ahead past the 'no entry' road sign. Follow this road to Oxenhope Station (22.5km). Go past the station entrance, onto the road running straight ahead. Cross the bridge and 100m further on follow the signpost to the left for the "Worth Valley Way". This path runs between a house and some shunting yards for the railway before disappearing through trees into pastureland.

Follow the yellow arrows along this footpath. It leads over a footbridge, and close to a level crossing over the railway line (do not cross the tracks). Continue following the yellow arrows past a farmhouse and back over the river. Continue along this side of the river bank for almost 2km, staying close to the river bank for most of the route and ignoring both footbridges that lead to the other side of the river. This is a delightful stretch of footpath along water meadows with a rich variety of vegetation. The train line is never far away and provides occasional opportunities to see the magnificent steam trains working their way along the valley. The path also passes under the new windmill that has been such a prominent landmark since Top of Stairs and, near the end of this stretch, passes an unusual house.

When the footpath eventually reaches the road turn left towards Haworth. After 20m the road swings around the right. Go straight on to the railway station and bus stops (25km) or go right and steeply uphill to find historic Haworth. Both ends of town provide plenty of refreshments and chance to relax after a long and enjoyable days walking.

Western Section – Walk Four

Haworth to Steeton

Route: Haworth – Lower Laithes Reservoir – Newsholme – Goose Eye – Laycock – Whitely Head – Steeton

Distance: 14.5km; 9ml

Time: 4 – 5$^1/_2$ hr

Ascent: 475m 1550ft

Maps: 1:25000 Outdoor Leisure (21) South Pennines. Pathfinder: (671) Keighley and Ilkley. 1:50000 Landranger: (104) Leeds, Bradford and Harrogate.

Getting There

There are many ways to get to Haworth. The most spectacular approach is by steam train from Keighley along the Worth Valley Railway Line. Trains run daily in July and August, but at weekends only throughout the rest of the year. There are also direct bus services to Howarth from Keighley and Bradford and an occasional service (500) from Hebden Bridge and Todmorden (see previous chapter for details of this route). If coming from Halifax or Huddersfield the 502 service to Keighley passes close to Haworth and you alight at Crossroads to walk or catch a bus for the last mile into the town.

The Day Ahead

This is a lovely day's walk, and though quite short, is still demanding because of the number of ascents involved. The walk starts from Haworth railway station with a stiff climb to the top of the town.

Haworth High Street

Passing through the centre of Howarth, the route runs past the church and the Brontë Parsonage Museum before leading into open countryside. It then drops to Lower Laithes reservoir. From here the route climbs and falls across several valleys, passing through the hamlets of Lumb Foot, Newsholme, Goose Eye and Laycock. Pubs are passed at Hare Hills Lane (between Lumb Foot and Newsholme) and Goose Eye. The climb from Goose Eye to Laycock is quite formidable. From the higher village, the route continues to climb gently, threading its way between gaps in the extensive dry stone walling. Cutshaw Moor is the last hill on the West Yorkshire Way and from here there are wonderful views over to Rombalds Moor (where the walk began) and the Dales beyond.

There are plenty of opportunities to break the walk into more than one day trip. Today's route crosses that of a local bus service (M6) at four points: on the road above Lower Laithes Reservoir; Hare Hill Lane; Goose Eye; and Laycock. This bus route runs on to Haworth in one direction and Keighley in the other.

From Haworth Railway Station

Go right from Haworth railway station and immediately right over the footbridge that leads over the railway line. This provides excellent views of the railway yards, with their complement of steam locomotives and historic carriages. Once over the bridge go up Butt Lane, the cobbled lane to the right that runs steeply uphill. It passes the park on your left and school playing fields on the right. Cross over the first road junction and follow the cobbled lane uphill as it swings to the right, leading to Haworth High Street. This is the heart of Brontë country, full of souvenir shops and day trippers. Go right at the junction and follow the street up past the church on the left to the Tourist Information Centre (1km). The first (and hardest) climb of the day is already completed.

Near the Tourist Information Centre take the footpath to the left, signposted for the Brontë Parsonage Museum. This takes you past the Kings Arms, the main entrance to the church, and a few metres further on, the museum itself. Continue past the museum, taking the path that runs straight ahead past some allotments, some houses and into a field. Follow the flagged footpath across the field to the gap in the wall in the bottom corner. Turn left onto the road and 100m further on, go left onto the road signposted for Penistone Hill. Follow this uphill for 300m,

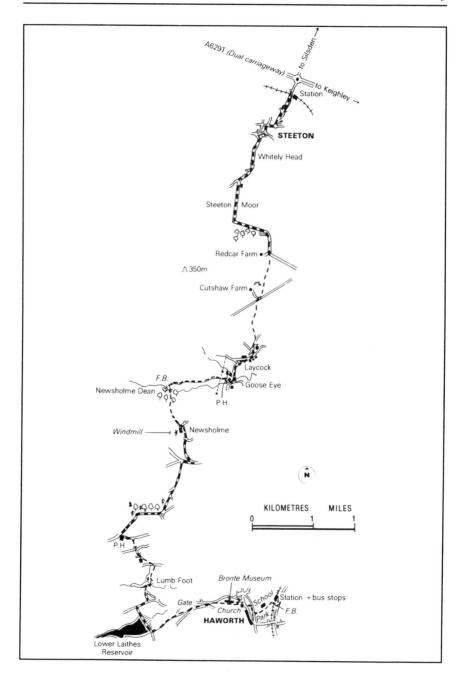

passing a car park on your right. Shortly after this, go right onto a track with a barrier across it, which leads towards Lower Laithes Reservoir. The reservoir becomes visible almost as soon as you pass the barrier and you follow the path all the way down to the road at the bottom (2km).

Turn right at the reservoir onto the road that runs across the the reservoir dam-wall and beyond, climbing to the road junction ahead. Go right here and follow the road downhill for 200m turning left onto the signposted footpath. This runs between two dry stone walls, descending gently at first then quite steeply towards the cottages at Lumb Foot (3km).

When the path meets a drive turn left and follow a sharp dog-leg in the drive. Continue along this drive which becomes a rougher track and then leads to the stream below. Make for the green footbridge over the stream and follow the path uphill through the woods, keeping close to the dry stone wall on your right. At the top of the woods go left onto the track (currently under construction) and 20m further on cross the stile on the right. Follow the path from here, crossing another stile along the way, to come to a farmhouse. Take the track to the right and follow this up to the road. Turn left onto the road and then, almost immediately, go right through a five-bar metal gate into a field (not signposted). Follow the dry stone wall uphill to Hare Hill Lane (4km).

Go left here and 200m along this road pass a Public House, The Grouse. Opposite this, there is an unmade track on the right; follow this track uphill towards the woods and continue for just over 0.5km to the first farm house. Immediately after this there is a junction of tracks. Take the left-hand track (White Lane), which runs uphill at first, but then begins to descend to the road ahead (6km). Go right and after 50m go left onto a minor road that starts to descend towards Newsholme. The road passes over a brook before climbing to the hamlet. One of the first buildings you pass is Church Farm with its unique windmill. Follow the road as it weaves its way through the hamlet, twisting first to the left and then to the right. After the last house on the left take the track on the left which soon becomes a green lane running between two dry stone walls. After 200m the track turns sharply left, carry straight on following the footpath ahead. This leads to a stile and then drops steeply into the valley below towards some woods and the bottom of Newsholme Dean (7km).

On reaching the valley bottom, go through a wooden gate and make for the footbridge ahead. There are two bridges here: the first one that you will see, although in a traditional style, is quite modern – 1989 being the date in the concrete. A few feet downstream there is a much older clapper bridge. Follow the path away from the stream, going through the white gate on the right. This leads to a track passing some cottages and climbing gently away from the valley bottom. Keep on this upper track for almost 1km until it rises more sharply and turns off to the left (8km). Just before the turn, take the narrow footpath to the right that drops down the side of the bank. After 300m this joins a wider track. Go left onto this and follow the track as it zig-zags around a bend to lead into Goose Eye. This is an extremely pretty village, well worth investigating. Just around the corner on the right there is an excellent Public House (The Turkey) and the remnants of an old mill. There are several interesting and tasteful conversions of old industrial buildings to be found in the village (8.5km)

The West Yorkshire Way turns left from where it enters Goose Eye and climbs up the formidable hill ahead. Near the top of the hill the road veers sharply to the left and you take the ginnel leading up to the houses above, at the edge of the village of Laycock. At the top of the lane turn right onto the road and 300m further on turn left into Chapel Lane. After 150m, take the track to the right which passes several houses before becoming a footpath running to a gate. Go through this and cut diagonally across this field to the gap in the top right corner. Cut across the next field heading for the gap in the middle of the top wall and then diagonally across the third field, looking for the gap in the wall on the right-hand side. Cut directly across the next three fields, where the gaps are all obvious and then diagonally across the top two fields, heading for the top right-hand corner of each. Passing through this last gap brings you out onto a road (9.5km).

On reaching the road turn right and look out for the signposted footpath 75m further on. The post is immediately next to the drive leading off to Cutshaw Farm. The start of this path isn't immediately obvious, just a dry stone wall with the top stones removed. Follow the path diagonally across this field to the top right-hand corner. Cut across the very corner of the next field, through the gap in the top of the wall, and then diagonally to the top right corner of the next field. The path has been climbing gently for the last 1km and here you reach the top of Cutshaw

Ginnel between Goose Eye and Laycock

Moor, with clear views over to Rombalds Moor and the Southern Dales. The view eastwards to where this walk began some 150 miles ago is one worth savouring – the more so, since this is the last hill on the West Yorkshire Way and it is all downhill from here to Steeton.

From this vantage point follow the path across the field to the gap in the wall on the right-hand side. Veer to the left in this field and follow the path to the stone stile that leads to the road. This stile is not too visible, but can be found some 50m to the right of the farm track running to Higher Redcar Farm on the left. Once onto the road turn left and follow it downhill for 2km. The road twists, first to the right, then to the left, then to the right again. After the third bend the road drops more steeply, passing some cottages and the village of Whitley Head (13km). Eventually the road drops down into Steeton. Follow it through the village to a green and turn left into Mill Lane. Go right at the main road and follow this for 200m to the second set of traffic lights. Go left here into Station Road and follow this for 500m to the railway station. Trains to Keighley and the rest of West Yorkshire depart from the far platform (14.5km).

Congratulations! You have just completed the West Yorkshire Way.

Route Planning on Public Transport

This table lays out the most direct routes to each of the starting points on the West Yorkshire Way from five major towns in the county. The letter "c" indicates where any changes need to be made (see below for abbreviations). Times given are approximate travel times that take connections into account. These are for guidance only and you should check with the appropriate bus or train timetables for the times when you want to travel.

FROM: TO:	LEEDS	BRADFORD	WAKEFIELD	HUDDERSFIELD	HALIFAX
Steeton	T 30min	T 30min	2T cLS 1hr 10min	2T cLS 1hr 15min	2T cLS 1hr 20m
Ilkley	T 30min	T 30min	2T cLS 1hr 15min	2T cLS 1hr 20min	2T cLS 1hr 25m
Bramhope	B 25min	T+B cLS 1hr 5min	T+B cLS 1hr	T+B cLS 1hr 20min	T+B cLS 1hr 20min
Wetherby	B 50min	T+B cLS 1hr 25min	T+B cLS 1hr 30min	T+B cLS 1hr 40min	T+B cLS 1hr 40min
EastGarforth	T 20min	T 40min	2T cLS 45min	2T cLS 50min	T 55min
Knottingley	T 35min	2T cLS 1hr 10min	T 30min	2T cWF 1hr 20min	2T cLS 2h
S. Elmsall	T 30min	2T cLS 1hr 15min	T 15min	2T cWF 1hr 10min	2T cLS 2h
Darton	T 45min	2T cLS 1hr 20min	T 10min	B 1hr	2T cLS 1hr 30min
DenbyDale	2T cHD 1hr 30min	2B cHD 2h	B 45min	T 25min	B+T cHD 1hr 10min
Holme	T+B cHD 1hr 40min	2B cHD 1hr 20min	2B cHF 1hr 40min	B 35min	2B cHD 1hr 10min
Marsden	2T cHD 55min	B+T cHD 1hr 20min	T 45min	T 15min	B+T cHD 1hr 15min
Todmorden	T 1hr	T 40min	2T cLS 1hr 30min	B+T cHX 1hr 20min	T 20min
Haworth*	2T cK 50min	B 45min	3T cLS,K 1hr 30min	2B cCR 1hr 50min	2B cCR 1hr 10min

KEY:
T – Direct Train. B – Direct Bus. 2T – Two Trains. 2B -Two buses.
T+B – Train and Bus. B+T – Bus and Train.

For Connections (c) the following code(s) apply
LS – Leeds. WF – Wakefield. HD – Huddersfield HF – Holmfirth.
HX – Halifax. K – Keighley. CR – Crossroads (near Howarth).

*Trains to Haworth operated by the Keighley and Worth Valley Railway

Index of Walks

	km	*ml*	*Ascent*
North			
Steeton to Ilkley	10	6.5	300m
Ilkley to Bramhope	17	10.5	420m
Bramhope to Wetherby	24	15	300m
Total	*51*	*32*	
East			
Wetherby to East Garforth	26	16	285m
East Garforth to Knottingley	17	10.5	150m
Knottingley to South Elmsall	23.5	14.5	180m
Total	*66.5*	*41.5*	
South			
South Elmsall to Darton	23	14.5	200m
Darton to Denby Dale	15	9.5	420m
Denby Dale to Holme	19	12	400m
Total	*57*	*36*	
West			
Holme to Marsden	13	8	280m
Marsden to Todmorden	24	15	450m
Todmorden to Howarth	25	15.5	720m
Howarth to Steeton	14.5	9	400m
Total	*76*	*47.5*	
GRAND TOTAL	*249.0*	*156.5*	

Useful Addresses

Transport Services

Metro have a series of offices throughout the county which can offer advice about public transport routes, timetables and prices. The main offices are at:

Bradford: 0274-732237

Halifax: 0422-364467

Huddersfield: 0484-545444

Leeds: 0532-457676

Wakefield: 0924-375555

Train timetables can be picked up at any main railway station in the county.

Tourist Information Centres

Tourist Information Centres can provide a wide range of information, including that of locally available accommodation. There are a dozen in the county, which are open all year.

Bradford: National Museum of Photography, Princes View; Tel 0274-75368

Halifax: Piece Hall; Tel 0422-368725

Haworth: 2-4 West Lane; Tel 0535 62329

Hebden Bridge: 1 Bridge Gate; Tel 0422-843831

Holmfirth: 49-51 Huddersfield Road; Tel 0484-687603/684992

Huddersfield: 3-5 Albion Street; Tel 0484-430808

Ilkley: Station Road; Tel 0943-602319

Leeds: 19 Wellington Street; Tel 0532-478301

Otley: Council Offices, 8 Boroughgate; Tel 0943-465151

Todmorden: 15 Burnley Road; Tel 0706-818181

Wakefield: Town Hall, Wood Street; Tel 0924-295000/1

Wetherby: Council Offices, 24 Westgate; Tel 0937-582706

Local Authority Countryside Services

Local Authority Countryside Services have a wealth of information (often free) about routes in their areas. The five Countryside Services within West Yorkshire can be contacted at the following addresses:

Bradford Countryside Services, Countryside House, Butt Lane, Haworth, BD 22 8QJ

Calderdale Countryside Services, Wellesley Park, Halifax HX2 0AY

Kirklees Countryside Services, High Street Buildings, High Street, Huddersfield HD1 2NQ

Leeds Countryside Services, Home Farm, Temple Newsome Park, Leeds LS15

Wakefield Countryside Services, 3rd Floor, Chantry House, 123 Kirkgate, Wakefield, WF1 1YG

Walking Organisations

There are several walking organisations and groups active within the area. This list provides national contacts, who will put you in contact with a local group.

Long Distance Walkers Association

Kevin Uzzell, Membership Secretary,
7 Ford Drive,
Yarnfield,
Stone,
Staffs ST15 0RP

The Ramblers Association

Membership Secretary,
1-5 Wandsworth Road,
London SW8 2XX

Explore the countryside with Sigma! Find out more about the north-west of England with our super guide books. We have a wide selection of guides to individual towns from Buxton to Lancaster, plus outdoor activities centred on walking and cycling in the great outdoors. Here are some recent highlights:

PEAK DISTRICT DIARY - Roger Redfern

An evocative book, celebrating the glorious countryside of the Peak District. The book is based on Roger's popular column in *The Guardian* newspaper and is profusely illustrated with stunning photographs. *£6.95*

I REMAIN, YOUR SON JACK - J. C. Morten (edited by Sheila Morten)

A collection of almost 200 letters, as featured on BBC TV, telling the moving story of a young soldier in the First World War. Profusely illustrated with contemporary photographs. *£8.95*

There are many books for outdoor people in our catalogue, including:

HERITAGE WALKS IN THE PEAK DISTRICT
- Clive Price

EAST CHESHIRE WALKS
- Graham Beech

WEST CHESHIRE WALKS
- Jen Darling

WEST PENNINE WALKS
- Mike Cresswell

NEWARK AND SHERWOOD RAMBLES
- Malcolm McKenzie

RAMBLES AROUND MANCHESTER
- Mike Cresswell

WESTERN LAKELAND RAMBLES
- Gordon Brown

WELSH WALKS: Dolgellau and the Cambrian Coast
- Laurence Main and Morag Perrott

WELSH WALKS: Aberystwyth and District
- Laurence Main and Morag Perrott

OFF-BEAT CYCLING IN THE PEAK DISTRICT
- Clive Smith

MORE OFF-BEAT CYCLING IN THE PEAK DISTRICT
- Clive Smith

50 BEST CYCLE RIDES IN CHESHIRE
- edited by Graham Beech

- all of these walking and cycling books are currently £6.95 each.

For long-distance walks enthusiasts, we have several books including:

THE GREATER MANCHESTER BOUNDARY WALK
- Graham Phythian

THE THIRLMERE WAY
- Tim Cappelli

THE MARCHES WAY
- Les Lumsdon

- all £6.95 each

We also publish:

A guide to the 'Pubs of Old Lancashire'

A fabulous series of 'Pub Walks' books all featuring access by public transport

A new series of investigations into the Supernatural, Myth and Magic

Superb illustrated books on Manchester's football teams

- plus many more entertaing and educational books being regularly added to our list.

All of our books are available from your local bookshop. In case of difficulty, or to obtain our complete catalogue, please contact:

Sigma Leisure,

1 South Oak Lane,

Wilmslow, Cheshire SK9 6AR

Phone: 0625 - 531035 Fax: 0625 - 536800

ACCESS and VISA orders welcome - call our friendly sales staff or use our 24 hour Answerphone service! Most orders are despatched on the day we receive your order - you could be enjoying our books in just a couple of days.

AUTHORS: if you have an interesting idea for a book, contact us for a rapid and expert decision. Note that we are not a 'Vanity Press' - all of our books earn royalties for their writers.

METRO DAYROVER. FROM £1.60 TO ANYWHERE YOU FANCY.*

With a Metro DayRover ticket, unlimited travel around West Yorkshire for one day by bus or train is a lot cheaper than you think.

Available from railway stations, bus stations, Metro Travel Centres and Post Offices, Metro DayRover prices range from just 80p for a child, £1.60 for a single adult to only £3.40 for the whole family.

So, there's never been a better time to have a day out with a Metro DayRover.

*Metro DayRover is not valid before 9.30am on Monday to Friday or on NightRider services or football specials.

Metro DayRover is valid in West Yorkshire only.

METRO
HERE TO GET YOU THERE